D0208961

A Gift For:

....

*The LORD is faithful to all his promises
and loving toward all he has made.*

PSALM 145:13

From:

....

God's Words
OF Life
For Women

ZONDERVAN®
.com

ZONDERVAN.com/
AUTHORTRACKER
follow your favorite authors

ISBN 978-0-310-33867-3

Printed in China

15 16 17 LEO 5

Contents
God's Words of Life on

CONTENTS

God's Words OF Life on

Accepting Others

Jesus said, "He who receives you receives me, and he who receives me receives the one who sent me."

Matthew 10:40

How good and pleasant it is
when brothers live together in unity!

Psalm 133:1

Jesus said, "Give to the one who asks you, and do not turn away from the one who wants to borrow from you. You have heard that it was said, 'Love your neighbor and hate your enemy.' But I tell you: Love your enemies and pray for those who persecute you."

Matthew 5:42–44

Jesus said, "To love [God] with all your heart, with all your understanding and with all your strength, and to love your neighbor as yourself is more important than all burnt offerings and sacrifices."

Mark 12:33

Jesus said, "Anyone who gives you a cup of water in my name because you belong to Christ will certainly not lose his reward."

Mark 9:41

Jesus said, "Do to others as you would have them do to you."

Luke 6:31

Jesus said, "I have set you an example that you should do as I have done for you."

John 13:15

Jesus said, "My command is this: Love each other as I have loved you. Greater love has no one than this, that he lay down his life for his friends."

John 15:12–13

Be devoted to one another in brotherly love. Honor one another above yourselves.

Romans 12:10

May the Lord make your love increase and overflow for each other and for everyone else, just as ours does for you.

1 Thessalonians 3:12

Let us consider how we may spur one another on toward love and good deeds.

Hebrews 10:24

If you really keep the royal law found in Scripture, "Love your neighbor as yourself," you are doing right.

James 2:8

Above all, love each other deeply, because love covers over a multitude of sins.

1 Peter 4:8

*A man of many companions may come to ruin,
but there is a friend who sticks closer
than a brother.*

Proverbs 18:24

And now, O Israel, what does the LORD your God ask of you but to fear the LORD your God, to walk in all his ways, to love him, to serve the LORD your God with all your heart and with all your soul . . . ?

Deuteronomy 10:12–13

Then Peter began to speak: "I now realize how true it is that God does not show favoritism but accepts men from every nation who fear him and do what is right."

Acts 10:34–35

How good and pleasant it is
when brothers live together in unity!

Psalm 133:1

For [Christ] himself is our peace.

Ephesians 2:14

He has showed you, O man, what is good.
And what does the LORD require of you?
To act justly and to love mercy
and to walk humbly with your God.

Micah 6:8

Devotional Thought on Accepting Others

Some people have a way of making themselves at home. They don't ring the front doorbell. They slip in the back. They don't care if there's clutter on the floor. They'll either help you pick it up, or step over it to pour you each a cup of coffee.

How do these people do it? Perhaps the key to the back door of our hearts is simply acceptance—the kind of love that would just as soon hug you in a tattered bathrobe as in your Sunday best.

Such people leave behind their expectations of how others should be and what they should do. To them, every person is buried treasure to be discovered and enjoyed. Differences are a source of delight. Evaluations, judgments, and makeovers are not their job. Loving acceptance is.

When such a person takes me into her heart, it is certain that she cannot stay long out of mine.

Susan Lenzkes

God's Words OF *Life on*

Anxiety

Cast your cares on the LORD
   and he will sustain you;
   he will never let the righteous fall.

Psalm 55:22

Commit your way to the LORD;
   trust in him and he will do this:
He will make your righteousness shine like the
   dawn, the justice of your cause like the
   noonday sun.

Psalm 37:5–6

Commit to the LORD whatever you do,
   and your plans will succeed.

Proverbs 16:3

Blessed is the man who trusts in the LORD,
whose confidence is in him.
He will be like a tree planted by the water
that sends out its roots by the stream.
It does not fear when heat comes;
its leaves are always green.
It has no worries in a year of drought and
never fails to bear fruit.

Jeremiah 17:7–8

Jesus said, "Look at the birds of the air; they do not sow or reap or store away in barns, and yet your heavenly Father feeds them. Are you not much more valuable than they?"

Matthew 6:26

Do not be anxious about anything, but in everything, by prayer and petition, with thanksgiving, present your requests to God. And the peace of God, which transcends all understanding, will guard your hearts and your minds in Christ Jesus.

Philippians 4:6–7

Jesus said, "Do you worry about clothes? See how the lilies of the field grow. They do not labor or spin. Yet I tell you that not even Solomon in all his splendor was dressed like one of these. If that is how God clothes the grass of the field, which is here today and tomorrow is thrown into the fire, will he not much more clothe you, O you of little faith?"

Matthew 6:28–30

Cast all your anxiety on [Jesus] because he cares for you.

1 Peter 5:7

Jesus said to his disciples: "Therefore I tell you, do not worry about your life, what you will eat; or about your body, what you will wear. Life is more than food, and the body more than clothes."

Luke 12:22–23

The LORD replied, "My Presence will go with you, and I will give you rest."

Exodus 33:14

Jesus said, "Do not be afraid, little flock, for your Father has been pleased to give you the kingdom."

Luke 12:32

The fruit of the Spirit is love, joy, peace, patience, kindness, goodness, faithfulness, gentleness and self-control.

Galatians 5:22–23

The LORD himself goes before you and will be with you; he will never leave you nor forsake you. Do not be afraid; do not be discouraged.

Deuteronomy 31:8

The Lord says, "Be strong and courageous. Do not be terrified; do not be discouraged, for the LORD your God will be with you wherever you go."

Joshua 1:9

Jesus said, "Come to me, all you who are weary and burdened, and I will give you rest. Take my yoke upon you and learn from me, for I am gentle and humble in heart, and you will find rest for your souls."

Matthew 11:28–29

Be transformed by the renewing of your mind. Then you will be able to test and approve what God's will is—his good, pleasing and perfect will.

Romans 12:2

God did not give us a spirit of timidity, but a spirit of power, of love and of self-discipline.

2 Timothy 1:7

He who fears the Lord has a secure fortress.
Proverbs 14:26

Let us then approach the throne of grace with confidence, so that we may receive mercy and find grace to help us in our time of need.

Hebrews 4:16

The LORD is with you when you are with him. If you seek him, he will be found by you.

2 Chronicles 15:2

> *The LORD gives strength to his people;*
>   *the LORD blesses his people with peace.*
> *Psalm 29:11*

Dear friends, let us love one another, for love comes from God. Everyone who loves has been born of God and knows God.

1 John 4:7

> *My flesh and my heart may fail,*
>   *but God is the strength of my heart*
>   *and my portion forever.*
> *Psalm 73:26*

> *Great peace have they who love*
>   *your law,*
>   *and nothing can make them stumble.*
> *Psalm 119:165*

Those who trust in the LORD are like Mount Zion,
which cannot be shaken but endures forever.

Psalm 125:1

In the day of my trouble I will call to you,
for you will answer me.

Psalm 86:7

God is able to make all grace abound to you, so that in all things at all times, having all that you need, you will abound in every good work.

2 Corinthians 9:8

Blessed is the man who trusts in the LORD,
whose confidence is in him.

Jeremiah 17:7

Let us not become weary in doing good, for at the proper time we will reap a harvest if we do not give up. Therefore, as we have opportunity, let us do good to all people, especially to those who belong to the family of believers.

Galatians 6:9–10

Devotional Thought on Anxiety

The story of Exodus is played out in miniature in the life of every believer.

Like the Jews of old, we are held in bondage. But God saves us from our enemy and leads us into freedom and into the promised land of his presence.

While we live on earth, we are involved in this exodus journey. We seem to wander in a desert of our own weakness and sin. Our faith is tested by difficulty. We have fears and anxieties, many of which are real. It is not only "the things that go bump in the night" that terrify us.

We sense an evil presence intent on overtaking us.

But like the Jewish people fleeing the wrath of Pharaoh, we can be certain that God will surround us with his protection. Though evil may threaten us, it will never overwhelm us. Surrounded by Christ, we will pass safely through this world to the next.

Ann Spangler

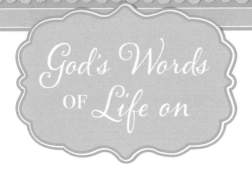

God's Words OF *Life on*

Beauty

A wife of noble character who can find?
She is worth far more than rubies.

Proverbs 31:10

Your beauty should not come from outward adorn-
ment, such as braided hair and the wearing of gold
jewelry and fine clothes. Instead, it should be that of
your inner self, the unfading beauty of a gentle and
quiet spirit, which is of great worth in God's sight. For
this is the way the holy women of the past who put
their hope in God used to make themselves beautiful.

1 Peter 3:3–5

One thing I ask of the LORD,
this is what I seek:

that I may dwell in the house of the LORD
all the days of my life,
to gaze upon the beauty of the LORD
and to seek him in his temple.

Psalm 27:4

Charm is deceptive, and beauty is fleeting;
but a woman who fears the
LORD *is to be praised.*

Proverbs 31:30

She is clothed with strength and dignity;
she can laugh at the days to come.
She speaks with wisdom,
and faithful instruction is on her tongue.

Proverbs 31:25–26

[God] has made everything beautiful in its time.

Ecclesiastes 3:11

Devotional Thought on Beauty

We all have imperfections. We live in an imperfect world.

Our created purpose is to let God's light shine through every facet of our being, expressing his colors and beauty through us in ways no one else can.

If you look at a ring under the microscope every day and become intimately familiar with every flaw, you might be embarrassed by it.

But that is not how God meant the beauty of diamonds to be seen. The beauty of a diamond is seen when someone holds it up in the sunlight, and everyone can see it sparkle.

We are created to shine with the light of God's creative genius. When you appreciate yourself in all your uniqueness, you will dare to hold your life up to the light. You will dare to live out the beauty you were created to express . . . cleaned and polished with the forgiveness of God.

Connie Neal

God's Words OF Life on

Changes

[God] has made everything beautiful in its time. He has also set eternity in the hearts of men; yet they cannot fathom what God has done from beginning to end. I know that there is nothing better for men than to be happy and do good while they live. That everyone may eat and drink, and find satisfaction in all his toil—this is the gift of God.

Ecclesiastes 3:11–13

When I was woven together in the depths of
the earth,
your eyes saw my unformed body.
All the days ordained for me
were written in your book before
one of them came to be.
How precious to me are your thoughts, O God!
How vast is the sum of them!

Were I to count them,
    they would outnumber the grains of sand.
When I awake, I am still with you.

Psalm 139:15–18

One thing I ask of the LORD,
    this is what I seek:
that I may dwell in the house of the LORD
    all the days of my life,
to gaze upon the beauty of the LORD
    and to seek him in his temple.

Psalm 27:4

I thought, "Age should speak;
    advanced years should teach wisdom."
But it is the spirit in a man,
    the breath of the Almighty,
        that gives him understanding.

Job 32:7–8

Even when I am old and gray,
    do not forsake me, O God,
till I declare your power to the next generation,
    your might to all who are to come.

Psalm 71:18

The LORD is upright;
*   he is my Rock, and there is no wickedness*
*   in him.*

Psalm 92:15

Young men and maidens,
*   old men and children.*
Let them praise the name of the LORD,
*   for his name alone is exalted;*
*   his splendor is above the*
*   earth and the heavens.*

Psalm 148:12–13

Gray hair is a crown of splendor;
*   it is attained by a righteous life.*

Proverbs 16:31

Remember your Creator
*   in the days of your youth,*
before the days of trouble come
*   and the years approach when*
*   you will say,*
*   "I find no pleasure in them."*

Ecclesiastes 12:1

Man's days are determined;
you have decreed the number
of his months
and have set limits he cannot exceed.

Job 14:5

The apostle John said, "I saw a new heaven and a new earth, for the first heaven and the first earth had passed away, and there was no longer any sea. I saw the Holy City, the new Jerusalem, coming down out of heaven from God, prepared as a bride beautifully dressed for her husband. And I heard a loud voice from the throne saying, 'Now the dwelling of God is with men, and he will live with them. They will be his people, and God himself will be with them and be their God. He will wipe every tear from their eyes. There will be no more death or mourning or crying or pain, for the old order of things has passed away.' He who was seated on the throne said, 'I am making everything new!'"

Revelation 21:1–5

He asked you for life, and you
gave it to him—
length of days, for ever and ever.

Psalm 21:4

Whoever of you loves life
    and desires to see many good days,
keep your tongue from evil
    and your lips from speaking lies.

Psalm 34:12–13

"With long life will I satisfy him
    and show him my salvation," says the
    Lord.

Psalm 91:16

Keep my commands in your heart,
for they will prolong your life many years
    and bring you prosperity.

Proverbs 3:1–2

Through me your days will be many,
    and years will be added to your life.

Proverbs 9:11

The fear of the LORD adds length to life.

Proverbs 10:27

Listen, I tell you a mystery: We will not all sleep, but
we will all be changed.

1 Corinthians 15:51

When I was a child, I talked like a child, I thought like a child, I reasoned like a child. When I became a man, I put childish ways behind me.

1 Corinthians 13:11

The eternal God is your refuge,
and underneath are the everlasting arms.
He will drive out your enemy before you,
saying, "Destroy him!"

Deuteronomy 33:27

"Even to your old age and gray hairs
I am he, I am he who will sustain you.
I have made you and I will carry you;
I will sustain you and I will
rescue you," says the Lord.

Isaiah 46:4

Devotional Thought on Changes

Here she stands, my mother for forty years. As I look at her, I sense that someone has wound the clock. Years have become increments. History has a beginning and an end. Then Mother's arms wrap me in warmth, and I am home. A forty-year-old child reassured by her mother's touch. There is no time in touch.

I hear the tea kettle whistling. Mother's chocolate chip cookies pull me back into timelessness. Our laughter drowns out the clock. There is no time in laughter.

For a moment I forget ticking clocks.

I am held together by things that do not change—a mother's early morning welcome, freshly baked chocolate chip cookies, an ironstone plate, and laughter.

I am held together by a God who does not change. I know the God of time who is yet above time. I see tonight in my mother's face the strange paradox of time and timelessness.

A rare glimpse of the divine.

Ruth Senter

Conflict

May the God who gives endurance and encouragement give you a spirit of unity among yourselves as
you follow Christ Jesus, so that with one heart and
mouth you may glorify the God and Father of our Lord
Jesus Christ. Accept one another, then, just as Christ
accepted you, in order to bring praise to God.

Romans 15:5–7

I appeal to you, brothers, in the name of our Lord Jesus
Christ, that all of you agree with one another so that
there may be no divisions among you and that you may
be perfectly united in mind and thought.

1 Corinthians 1:10

Whatever happens, conduct yourselves in a manner
worthy of the gospel of Christ. Then, . . . I will know

that you stand firm in one spirit, contending as one for the faith of the gospel.

Philippians 1:27

Make my joy complete by being like-minded, having the same love, being one in spirit and purpose. Do nothing out of selfish ambition or vain conceit, but in humility consider others better than yourselves. Each of you should look not only to your own interests, but also to the interests of others.

Philippians 2:2–4

Live in harmony with one another; be sympathetic, love as brothers, be compassionate and humble. Do not repay evil with evil or insult with insult, but with blessing, because to this you were called so that you may inherit a blessing.

1 Peter 3:8–9

"Love your neighbor as yourself. I am the LORD."

Leviticus 19:18

Let us . . . make every effort to do what leads to peace and to mutual edification.

Romans 14:19

Refrain from anger and turn from wrath;
do not fret—it leads only to evil.
Psalm 37:8

A gentle answer turns away wrath.
Proverbs 15:1

Do not be overcome by evil, but overcome evil with good.
Romans 12:21

A fool shows his annoyance at once,
but a prudent man overlooks an insult.
Proverbs 12:16

A gentle answer turns away wrath,
but a harsh word stirs up anger.
Proverbs 15:1

A hot-tempered man stirs up dissension,
but a patient man calms a quarrel.
Proverbs 15:18

Starting a quarrel is like breaching a dam;
so drop the matter before a dispute
breaks out.
Proverbs 17:14

A man's wisdom gives him patience;
it is to his glory to overlook an offense.
Proverbs 19:11

Do not make friends with a hot-tempered man,
do not associate with one easily angered,
or you may learn his ways
and get yourself ensnared.
Proverbs 22:24–25

As a prisoner for the Lord, then, I urge you to live a life worthy of the calling you have received. Be completely humble and gentle; be patient, bearing with one another in love. Make every effort to keep the unity of the Spirit through the bond of peace.

Ephesians 4:1–3

Get rid of all bitterness, rage and anger, brawling and slander, along with every form of malice. Be kind and compassionate to one another, forgiving each other, just as in Christ God forgave you.

Ephesians 4:31–32

Do not let the sun go down while you are still angry, and do not give the devil a foothold.

Ephesians 4:26–27

My dear brothers, take note of this: Everyone should be quick to listen, slow to speak and slow to become angry, for man's anger does not bring about the righteous life that God desires.

James 1:19–20

Jesus said, "Love your enemies and pray for those who persecute you."

Matthew 5:44

Hatred stirs up dissension,
but love covers over all wrongs.

Proverbs 10:12

Let your gentleness be evident to all.

Philippians 4:5

Love is patient, love is kind. It does not envy, it does not boast, it is not proud. It is not rude, it is not self-seeking, it is not easily angered, it keeps no record of wrongs.

1 Corinthians 13:4–5

How good and pleasant it is
when brothers live together in unity!

Psalm 133:1

Jesus said, "Blessed are the peacemakers, for they will be called sons of God."

Matthew 5:9

Devotional Thought on Conflict

The secret to unity? Taking the other person's needs, feelings, and desires into yourself.

Unity is wonderful when it happens, but it's often difficult to achieve. Believers differ, disagree, hurt each other's feelings, fight about issues and problems.

The key to becoming one lies in Jesus' prayer to his Father for all believers: "that they may be one as we are one: I in them and you in me" (John 17:22–23).

Do you willingly pledge yourself to put Jesus' plans and priorities first, making them your own? Then you have allowed Jesus to be "in" you.

And when you meet with other believers who have done the same, you can't help but become "like-minded, having the same love, being one in spirit and purpose" (Philippians 2:2).

Edith Bajema

God's Words OF Life on

Contentment

LORD, *you have assigned me my portion and*
        my cup;
    you have made my lot secure.
The boundary lines have fallen
        for me in pleasant places;
    surely I have a delightful inheritance.
                                        Psalm 16:5–6

Be still before the LORD
    and wait patiently for him;
do not fret when men succeed in their ways,
    when they carry out their wicked schemes.
Refrain from anger and turn from wrath;
    do not fret—it leads only to evil.
For evil men will be cut off,

but those who hope in the LORD
will inherit the land.

Psalm 37:7–9

Better the little that the righteous have
than the wealth of many wicked;
for the power of the wicked will be broken,
but the LORD upholds the righteous.

Psalm 37:16–17

[The LORD] fulfills the desires of those who
fear him;
he hears their cry and saves them.

Psalm 145:19

The faithless will be fully repaid for their ways,
and the good man rewarded for his.

Proverbs 14:14

A happy heart makes the face cheerful.

Proverbs 15:13

Better a little with the fear of the LORD
than great wealth with turmoil.
Better a meal of vegetables where there is love
than a fattened calf with hatred.

Proverbs 15:16–17

A cheerful look brings joy to the heart,
and good news gives health to the bones.

Proverbs 15:30

Better a little with righteousness
than much gain with injustice.

Proverbs 16:8

Better a dry crust with peace and quiet
than a house full of feasting, with strife.

Proverbs 17:1

I know that there is nothing better for men than to be happy and do good while they live. That everyone may eat and drink, and find satisfaction in all his toil—this is the gift of God.

Ecclesiastes 3:12–13

Better one handful with tranquility
than two handfuls with toil
and chasing after the wind.

Ecclesiastes 4:6

I commend the enjoyment of life, because nothing is better for a man under the sun than to eat and drink and be glad. Then joy will accompany him in his work all the days of the life God has given him under the sun.

Ecclesiastes 8:15

Trust in the LORD *with all your heart*
and lean not on your own understanding;
in all your ways acknowledge him,
and he will make your paths straight.

Proverbs 3:5–6

I have learned to be content whatever the circumstances. I know what it is to be in need, and I know what it is to have plenty. I have learned the secret of being content in any and every situation, whether well fed or hungry, whether living in plenty or in want. I can do everything through Christ who gives me strength.

Philippians 4:11–13

Godliness with contentment is great gain. For we brought nothing into the world, and we can take nothing out of it. But if we have food and clothing, we will be content with that.

1 Timothy 6:6–8

Keep your lives free from the love of money and be content with what you have, because God has said,
"Never will I leave you;
never will I forsake you."
So we say with confidence,
"The Lord is my helper; I will not
be afraid."

Hebrews 13:5–6

Devotional Thought on Contentment

For most of life, I think we fight God.

We keep trying to show him what we were made for. We keep giving him better ideas.

We keep working for something bigger and greater than anything he seems to have in mind for many of us. By the time we are in midlife, we feel we somehow have missed out on some of the great things we were born for. We fight with God over this.

I come to you, however, knowing God made me not to impress you. Not to be perfect or a genius. Not to make a million dollars!

God made me to be uncomplicated in my faith. To watch children and kites and sunsets and rainbows and enjoy them. To take your hand regardless of who you are or how you look. To listen to you. To accept you right where you are. To love you unconditionally.

God made me to be real. To be honest.

To be open. To never compare myself to you, but to strive to become my own best person.

Ann Kiemel Anderson

God's Words
OF Life on

Creativity

God said to Moses, "I have chosen Bezalel . . . and I
have filled him with the Spirit of God, with skill, ability
and knowledge in all kinds of crafts—to make artistic
designs for work in gold, silver and bronze, to cut and
set stones, to work in wood, and to engage in all kinds
of craftsmanship. . . . Also I have given skill to all the
craftsmen to make everything I have commanded you."

Exodus 31:2–6

Every good and perfect gift is from above, coming
down from the Father of the heavenly lights, who does
not change like shifting shadows.

James 1:17

[A wife of noble character] makes
coverings for her bed;
she is clothed in fine linen and purple. . . .
She makes linen garments and sells them,
and supplies the merchants with sashes.
Proverbs 31:22, 24

Each one should use whatever gift he has received to serve others, faithfully administering God's grace in its various forms. If anyone speaks, he should do it as one speaking the very words of God. If anyone serves, he should do it with the strength God provides, so that in all things God may be praised through Jesus Christ. To him be the glory and the power for ever and ever. Amen.
1 Peter 4:10–11

The LORD God is a sun and shield;
the LORD bestows favor and honor;
no good thing does he withhold
from those whose walk is blameless.
Psalm 84:11

To the man who pleases him, God gives wisdom, knowledge and happiness.
Ecclesiastes 2:26

[God] changes times and seasons;
he sets up kings and deposes them.
He gives wisdom to the wise
and knowledge to the discerning.

Daniel 2:21

We have different gifts, according to the grace given us. If a man's gift is prophesying, let him use it in proportion to his faith. If it is serving, let him serve; if it is teaching, let him teach; if it is encouraging, let him encourage; if it is contributing to the needs of others, let him give generously; if it is leadership, let him govern diligently; if it is showing mercy, let him do it cheerfully.

Romans 12:6–8

In [Christ] you have been enriched in every way—in all your speaking and in all your knowledge.

1 Corinthians 1:5

Each man has his own gift from God; one has this gift, another has that.

1 Corinthians 7:7

If the willingness is there, the gift is acceptable according to what one has, not according to what he does not have.

2 Corinthians 8:12

There are different kinds of gifts, but the same Spirit. There are different kinds of service, but the same Lord. There are different kinds of working, but the same God works all of them in all men.

1 Corinthians 12:4–6

Each one should use whatever gift he has received to serve others, faithfully administering God's grace in its various forms.

1 Peter 4:10

I will sing and make music with all my soul.
Psalm 108:1

Devotional Thought on Creativity

I've heard it a million times—expressed with admiration and usually a little envy: "Oh, she's so creative."

Usually it describes an "artsy" kind of person—someone who paints or writes or makes pottery. Such creative pursuits can bring great joy to those who do them and to those who enjoy the results. But you really don't have to be an artist to infuse your home and life with the spirit of creativity.

Creativity is a God-given ability to take something ordinary and make it into something special. It is an openness to doing old things in new ways and a willingness to adapt other people's good ideas to suit our personal needs. And creativity is an ability we all possess, although many of us keep it hidden in the deep corners of our lives.

The creative spirit is part of our heritage as children of the One who created all things. And nurturing our creativity is part of our responsibility as stewards of God's good gifts.

Emilie Barnes

Depression

Cast your cares on the LORD
and he will sustain you;
he will never let the righteous fall.

Psalm 55:22

The eyes of the LORD are on the righteous
and his ears are attentive to their cry.

Psalm 34:15

Do not be anxious about anything, but in everything, by prayer and petition, with thanksgiving, present your requests to God.

And the peace of God, which transcends all understanding, will guard your hearts and your minds in Christ Jesus. Finally . . . whatever is true, whatever is

noble, whatever is right, whatever is pure, whatever is
lovely, whatever is admirable—if anything is excellent
or praiseworthy—think about such things.

Philippians 4:6–8

In my alarm I said,
"I am cut off from your sight!"
Yet you heard my cry for mercy
when I called to you for help.

Psalm 31:22

My tears have been my food
day and night,
while men say to me all day long,
"Where is your God?" . . .
Why are you downcast, O my soul?
Why so disturbed within me?
Put your hope in God,
for I will yet praise him,
my Savior and my God.

Psalm 42:3, 5–6

Let the morning bring me word
of your unfailing love, [LORD,]
for I have put my trust in you.
Show me the way I should go,
for to you I lift up my soul.

Psalm 143:8

"I will build them up and not tear them down; I will plant them and not uproot them. I will give them a heart to know me, that I am the LORD. They will be my people, and I will be their God, for they will return to me with all their heart."

Jeremiah 24:6–7

The LORD is a refuge for the oppressed,
a stronghold in times of trouble.

Psalm 9:9

The eternal God is your refuge,
and underneath are the everlasting arms.

Deuteronomy 33:27

God is our refuge and strength,
an ever-present help in trouble.
Therefore we will not fear,
though the earth give way
and the mountains fall into
the heart of the sea,
though its waters roar and foam
and the mountains quake
with their surging.

Psalm 46:1–3

If the LORD delights in a man's way,
*   he makes his steps firm;*
though he stumble, he will not fall,
*   for the LORD upholds him with his hand.*
                                    Psalm 37:23–24

I sought the LORD, and he answered me;
*   he delivered me from all my fears.*
                                    Psalm 34:4

The LORD is close to the brokenhearted
*   and saves those who are crushed in spirit.*
A righteous man may have many troubles,
*   but the LORD delivers him from them all.*
                                    Psalm 34:18–19

My soul finds rest in God alone;
*   my salvation comes from him.*
He alone is my rock and my salvation;
*   he is my fortress, I will never be shaken.*
                                    Psalm 62:1–2

My flesh and my heart may fail,
*   but God is the strength of my heart*
*   and my portion forever.*
                                    Psalm 73:26

When I said, "My foot is slipping,"
     your love, O LORD, supported me.
When anxiety was great within me,
     your consolation brought joy to my soul.
                    Psalm 94:18–19

The LORD upholds all those who fall
     and lifts up all who are bowed down.
                    Psalm 145:14

[God] gives strength to the weary
     and increases the power of the weak.
Even youths grow tired and weary,
     and young men stumble and fall;
but those who hope in the LORD
     will renew their strength.
They will soar on wings like eagles;
     they will run and not grow weary,
     they will walk and not be faint.
                    Isaiah 40:29–31

"I am the LORD, your God,
     who takes hold of your right hand
and says to you, Do not fear;
     I will help you."

                    Isaiah 41:13

> Men are not cast off
>   by the Lord forever.
> Though he brings grief, he will show compassion,
>   so great is his unfailing love.
>
> *Lamentations 3:31–32*

Jesus said, "Come to me, all you who are weary and burdened, and I will give you rest. Take my yoke upon you and learn from me, for I am gentle and humble in heart, and you will find rest for your souls."

Matthew 11:28–29

Jesus said, "Do not let your hearts be troubled. Trust in God; trust also in me."

John 14:1

"I will refresh the weary and satisfy the faint," says the Lord.

Jeremiah 31:25

Jesus said, "Peace I leave with you; my peace I give you. I do not give to you as the world gives. Do not let your hearts be troubled and do not be afraid."

John 14:27

Jesus said, "In this world you will have trouble. But take heart! I have overcome the world."

John 16:33

Devotional Thought on Depression

Here I sit. A rainy weekday morning.

The dreariness is contagious. I know the rain is good for farmers and plants. But I'm not a farmer and unlike plants, the rain dampens my spirit, not my roots.

How do we muster any enthusiasm on days like today? Days of downcast spirits, a heavy heart, and responsibilities that feel overwhelming? I wonder what bounty can be found in rainy days, dreary skies, and melancholy moods?

The answer softly comes to me—reassurance. Reassurance that I'm not in this alone. I'm starting in the right place. I'm coming to a moment of quiet and seeking the presence of God. Only he can bring order to my confusion, encouragement to my work-weary world, and enthusiasm to my dreary heart.

So, God, this one's for you. This day and all that lays before me I put in your hands.

The rain. The fatigue. The responsibilities.

The part of me that feels stretched beyond my limits. This day I give to you, knowing your limits are infinite and your love is inexhaustible.

Debra Klingsporn

God's Words OF Life on

Disappointment

You are my hiding place;
   you will protect me from trouble
   and surround me with songs of deliverance.
                    Psalm 32:7

Jesus said, "Blessed are those who mourn,
   for they will be comforted."
                    Matthew 5:4

Those who know your name will trust in you,
   for you, LORD, have never
   forsaken those who seek you.
                    Psalm 9:10

Jesus said, "Blessed are you who hunger now,
for you will be satisfied.
Blessed are you who weep now,
for you will laugh."

Luke 6:21

The eyes of the LORD are on those who fear him,
on those whose hope is in his unfailing love.

Psalm 33:18

When times are good, be happy;
but when times are bad, consider:
God has made the one as well as the other.

Ecclesiastes 7:14

Trust in him at all times, O people;
pour out your hearts to him,
for God is our refuge.

Psalm 62:8

Devotional Thought on Disappointment

We said we'd never grow up and we'd never grow old; we'd never trust anyone over thirty. And now some of us have long since passed that tender age.

For this generation, the twenty-five years between youth and middle-age have been marked by unmet expectations. We found many of our dreams unreachable. Growing up has been less about realizing our dreams and more about making our dreams subject to reality. Now we plow through time, groping, learning, hurting, struggling, failing, and sometimes succeeding.

Perhaps disappointed dreams are our best opportunities to transfer hope to its rightful place. Heaven is where our biggest dreams belong. Realizing that can help us make it through the here and now without placing a burden on the present that it was never meant to bear. That's hope—realistic hope—which may yet serve to carry us through the rest of the journey.

Paula Rinehart

God's Words
OF Life on

Discipleship

Jesus said, "Whoever finds his life will lose it, and whoever loses his life for my sake will find it."

Matthew 10:39

Jesus said, "His sheep follow him because they know his voice."

John 10:4

Lord, who may dwell in your sanctuary?
Who may live on your holy hill?
He whose walk is blameless
and who does what is righteous,
who speaks the truth from his heart.

Psalm 15:1–2

Since we are surrounded by such a great cloud of witnesses, let us throw off everything that hinders and the sin that so easily entangles, and let us run with perseverance the race marked out for us. Let us fix our eyes on Jesus, the author and perfecter of our faith, who for the joy set before him endured the cross, scorning its shame, and sat down at the right hand of the throne of God. Consider him who endured such opposition from sinful men, so that you will not grow weary and lose heart.

Hebrews 12:1–3

I have been crucified with Christ and I no longer live, but Christ lives in me. The life I live in the body, I live by faith in the Son of God, who loved me and gave himself for me.

Galatians 2:20

He follows my decrees
and faithfully keeps my laws.
That man is righteous;
he will surely live,
declares the Sovereign LORD.

Ezekiel 18:9

He has showed you, O man, what is good.
And what does the LORD *require of you?*

To act justly and to love mercy
and to walk humbly with your God.

Micah 6:8

Jesus said, "If anyone loves me, he will obey my teaching. My Father will love him, and we will come to him and make our home with him."

John 14:23

Jesus said, "Remain in me, and I will remain in you. No branch can bear fruit by itself; it must remain in the vine. Neither can you bear fruit unless you remain in me. I am the vine; you are the branches. If a man remains in me and I in him, he will bear much fruit; apart from me you can do nothing."

John 15:4–5

Those who live in accordance with the Spirit have their minds set on what the Spirit desires.

Romans 8:5

The one who sows to please the Spirit, from the Spirit will reap eternal life. Let us not become weary in doing good, for at the proper time we will reap a harvest if we do not give up.

Galatians 6:8–9

One thing I do: Forgetting what is behind and straining toward what is ahead, I press on toward the goal to win the prize for which God has called me heavenward in Christ Jesus.

Philippians 3:13–14

The grace of God that brings salvation has appeared to all men. It teaches us to say "No" to ungodliness and worldly passions, and to live self-controlled, upright and godly lives in this present age.

Titus 2:11–12

Religion that God our Father accepts as pure and faultless is this: to look after orphans and widows in their distress and to keep oneself from being polluted by the world.

James 1:27

Jesus said, "By this all men will know that you are my disciples, if you love one another."

John 13:35

Devotional Thought on Discipleship

Jesus invites us to be his disciples. If we choose to accept his loving invitation, we must understand that there are certain conditions to be fulfilled.

One of them is a willingness to accept the cross. Is this a once-for-all taking up of one particular burden? I don't think so. It seems to me that my "cross" is each particular occasion when I am given the chance to "die"—that is, to offer up my own will whenever it crosses Christ's.

It is never easy for me. Shall I make excuses for myself —that's the way I am; it's my personality; it's the way I was raised; I'm tired; I can't hack it; you don't understand—or shall I pick up this cross? When Jesus took up his cross, he was saying yes with all his being to the will of the Father. If I am unwilling to say yes in even a very little thing, how shall I accept a more painful thing?

The call still comes to us: *Take up your cross and come with me.* With you, Lord? *Yes, with me.* Will you give me strength and show me the way? *That was my promise—is it my custom to break promises?*

Elisabeth Elliot

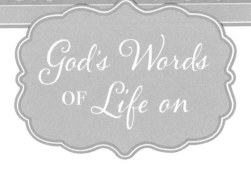

Encouragement

May our Lord Jesus Christ himself and God our Father, who loved us and by his grace gave us eternal encouragement and good hope, encourage your hearts and strengthen you in every good deed and word.

2 Thessalonians 2:16–17

This I call to mind
    and therefore I have hope:
Because of the LORD's great love we are not
        consumed,
    for his compassions never fail.
They are new every morning;
    great is your faithfulness.

Lamentations 3:21–23

And let us consider how we may spur one another on toward love and good deeds.

Hebrews 10:24

God, who has called you into fellowship with his Son Jesus Christ our Lord, is faithful.

1 Corinthians 1:9

The LORD is good to those whose hope is in him,
to the one who seeks him.

Lamentations 3:25

An anxious heart weighs a man down,
but a kind word cheers him up.

Proverbs 12:25

Devotional Thought on Encouragement

So many times in the past few weeks I had come home to hear a message of encouragement on my answering machine: "Thinking of you." "I love you." Day after day, when hysteria and raw emotions were my constant companions, I found the incredible support and concern of friends every time I needed someone.

Encouragement has never filled a flat tire. Encouragement has never made a car payment, nor fixed a broken washing machine. But encouragement from another gives us the strength to do what we feel we cannot do, hold on when we feel we cannot hold on, and try what we might not dare to try.

Encouragement. Doesn't sound like much, but it's everything. Send some encouragement today. You'll be part of someone's memories for a long, long time.

Sharon Mahoe

God's Words
OF Life on

Eternal Life

God has given us eternal life, and this life is in his Son.
He who has the Son has life; he who does not have the
Son of God does not have life.

1 John 5:11–12

Jesus said, "I tell you the truth, whoever hears my word
and believes him who sent me has eternal life and will not
be condemned; he has crossed over from death to life."

John 5:24

Jesus said, "For God so loved the world that he gave
his one and only Son, that whoever believes in him
shall not perish but have eternal life."

John 3:16

Jesus said, "I tell you the truth, he who believes has everlasting life."

John 6:47

Jesus said, "I am the living bread that came down from heaven. If anyone eats of this bread, he will live forever. This bread is my flesh, which I will give for the life of the world."

John 6:51

Jesus said, "Whoever drinks the water I give him will never thirst. Indeed, the water I give him will become in him a spring of water welling up to eternal life."

John 4:14

> *Surely goodness and love will follow me*
> *all the days of my life,*
> *and I will dwell in the house of the LORD*
> *forever.*

Psalm 23:6

The wages of sin is death, but the gift of God is eternal life in Christ Jesus our Lord.

Romans 6:23

Jesus said, "I am the resurrection and the life.
He who believes in me will live, even though he dies;
and whoever lives and believes in me will never die."

John 11:25–26

Jesus answered, "My sheep listen to my voice;
I know them, and they follow me. I give them eternal
life, and they shall never perish; no one can snatch them
out of my hand."

John 10:27–28

My soul finds rest in God alone;
my salvation comes from him.
He alone is my rock and my salvation;
he is my fortress, I will never be shaken. . . .
Find rest, O my soul, in God alone;
my hope comes from him. . . .
My salvation and my honor depend on God;
he is my mighty rock, my refuge.

Psalm 62:1–2, 5, 7

God will redeem my life from the grave;
he will surely take me to himself.

Psalm 49:15

Praise be to the God and Father of our Lord Jesus Christ! In his great mercy he has given us new birth into a living hope through the resurrection of Jesus Christ from the dead.

1 Peter 1:3

If you confess with your mouth, "Jesus is Lord," and believe in your heart that God raised him from the dead, you will be saved.

Romans 10:9

> *I trust in your unfailing love;*
>   *my heart rejoices in your salvation.*
> *I will sing to the LORD,*
>   *for he has been good to me.*

Psalm 13:5–6

Devotional Thought on Eternal Life

O Jesus Christ, the Bridegroom
Thou spotless Lamb of God
How all creation praises
How man and angels laud;
The heavenly hall is sounding
Redemption's antiphon
Bright majesty and glory
Stream from thy glorious throne.
And how the heart is raptured
With songs unto the Lamb
Upon the throne of heaven
Beside the great I Am;
His countenance of beauty
The raptured saint shall see
And never more grow weary
Through all eternity.
My soul within is longing
God's heav'n above to see
The home of all the Blessed
The dwelling of the free;
The Father, Son and Spirit
Invite the Bride to come
To that fair spotless Kingdom
Where love shall make all one.

Basilea Schlink

God's Words OF Life on

Faith

Since we have been justified through faith, we have peace with God through our Lord Jesus Christ.

Romans 5:1

Faith is being sure of what we hope for and certain of what we do not see.

Hebrews 11:1

Make every effort to add to your faith goodness; and to goodness, knowledge; and to knowledge, self-control; and to self-control, perseverance; and to perseverance, godliness; and to godliness, brotherly kindness; and to brotherly kindness, love. For if you possess these qualities in increasing measure, they will keep you from being ineffective and unproductive in your knowledge of our Lord Jesus Christ.

2 Peter 1:5–8

Faith comes from hearing the message, and the message is heard through the word of Christ.

Romans 10:17

Then Jesus answered, "Woman, you have great faith! Your request is granted." And her daughter was healed from that very hour.

Matthew 15:28

Let us fix our eyes on Jesus, the author and perfecter of our faith, who for the joy set before him endured the cross, scorning its shame, and sat down at the right hand of the throne of God.

Hebrews 12:2

Jesus replied, "I tell you the truth, if you have faith as small as a mustard seed, you can say to this mountain, 'Move from here to there' and it will move. Nothing will be impossible for you."

Matthew 17:20

"Have faith in God," Jesus answered. "I tell you the truth, if anyone says to this mountain, 'Go, throw yourself into the sea,' and does not doubt in his heart but believes that what he says will happen, it will be done for him. Therefore I tell you, whatever you ask for in prayer, believe that you have received it, and it will be yours."

Mark 11:22–24

We always thank God, the Father of our Lord Jesus Christ, when we pray for you, because we have heard of your faith in Christ Jesus and of the love you have for all the saints—the faith and love that spring from the hope that is stored up for you in heaven and that you have already heard about in the word of truth.

Colossians 1:3–5

We live by faith, not by sight.

2 Corinthians 5:7

Without faith it is impossible to please God, because anyone who comes to him must believe that he exists and that he rewards those who earnestly seek him.

Hebrews 11:6

These [trials] have come so that your faith—of greater worth than gold, which perishes even though refined by fire—may be proved genuine and may result in praise, glory and honor when Jesus Christ is revealed. Though you have not seen him, you love him; and even though you do not see him now, you believe in him and are filled with an inexpressible and glorious joy, for you are receiving the goal of your faith, the salvation of your souls.

1 Peter 1:7–9

I pray that out of his glorious riches he may strengthen you with power through his Spirit in your inner being, so that Christ may dwell in your hearts through faith. And I pray that you, being rooted and established in love, may have power, together with all the saints, to grasp how wide and long and high and deep is the love of Christ, and to know this love that surpasses knowledge—that you may be filled to the measure of all the fullness of God.

Ephesians 3:16–19

Devotional Thought on Faith

Without faith it is impossible to please God. I have experienced that having this kind of faith means being active, not sitting back bemoaning life and waiting for change.

It means loving and believing in ourselves and using the transforming power of God's Holy Spirit to move our lives forward.

The truth seems simple, but living it is not so simple. As time has gone by, I have seen the work of the Holy Spirit in my life. Times have been difficult financially, physically, mentally, and spiritually, but faith in God has begun a revolution in my life. Our enemy is fear that blinds us to truth, fear that keeps us bitter with anger, and fear that leaves us without power.

However, with renewed faith we are never alone. We realize that in Christ we have everything we need to overcome any of life's challenges. There may have been countless times when we have felt the earth shake beneath us, or the weight of life pressing in on us. This is happening to people today and to people throughout the world. It is one of the many ways in which the Holy Spirit speaks to us and encourages us to change.

Deneese L. Jones

God's Words
OF Life on

Finances

The LORD is my shepherd, I shall not be in want.
Psalm 23:1

[O LORD,] turn my heart toward your statutes
and not toward selfish gain.
Psalm 119:36

Jesus said, "No one can serve two masters. Either he will hate the one and love the other, or he will be devoted to the one and despise the other. You cannot serve both God and Money."

Matthew 6:24

Whoever trusts in his riches will fall,
but the righteous will thrive
like a green leaf.

Proverbs 11:28

Godliness with contentment is great gain. For we brought nothing into the world, and we can take nothing out of it. But if we have food and clothing, we will be content with that.

1 Timothy 6:6–8

I know what it is to be in need, and I know what it is to have plenty. I have learned the secret of being content in any and every situation, whether well fed or hungry, whether living in plenty or in want. I can do everything through him who gives me strength.

Philippians 4:12–13

Jesus sat down opposite the place where the offerings were put and watched the crowd putting their money into the temple treasury. Many rich people threw in large amounts. But a poor widow came and put in two very small copper coins, worth only a fraction of a penny. Calling his disciples to him, Jesus said, "I tell you the truth, this poor widow has put more into the treasury than all the others. They all gave out of their wealth; but she, out of her poverty, put in everything—all she had to live on."

Mark 12:41–44

"Bring the whole tithe into the storehouse, that there may be food in my house. Test me in this," says the

LORD Almighty, "and see if I will not throw open the floodgates of heaven and pour out so much blessing that you will not have room enough for it."

Malachi 3:10

Jesus said, "Watch out! Be on your guard against all kinds of greed; a man's life does not consist in the abundance of his possessions."

Luke 12:15

Jesus said, "Give, and it will be given to you. A good measure, pressed down, shaken together and running over, will be poured into your lap. For with the measure you use, it will be measured to you."

Luke 6:38

Let no debt remain outstanding, except the continuing debt to love one another, for he who loves his fellow-man has fulfilled the law.

Romans 13:8

Jesus said, "So do not worry, saying, 'What shall we eat?' or 'What shall we drink?' or 'What shall we wear?' For the pagans run after all these things, and your heavenly Father knows that you need them. But seek first his kingdom and his righteousness, and all these things will be given to you as well."

Matthew 6:31–33

Keep your lives free from the love of money and be content with what you have, because God has said,
> "Never will I leave you;
>> never will I forsake you."

Hebrews 13:5

Remember the LORD your God, for it is he who gives you the ability to produce wealth.

Deuteronomy 8:18

My God will meet all your needs according to his glorious riches in Christ Jesus.

Philippians 4:19

God is able to make all grace abound to you, so that in all things at all times, having all that you need, you will abound in every good work.

2 Corinthians 9:8

> A generous man will prosper;
>> he who refreshes others will himself be
>> refreshed.

Proverbs 11:25

Jesus said, "Store up for yourselves treasures in heaven, where moth and rust do not destroy, and where thieves do not break in and steal. For where your treasure is, there your heart will be also."

Matthew 6:20–21

A greedy man stirs up dissension,
but he who trusts in the LORD *will prosper.*
Proverbs 28:25

The Lord says, "Do not let this Book of the Law depart from your mouth; meditate on it day and night, so that you may be careful to do everything written in it. Then you will be prosperous and successful."

Joshua 1:8

Devotional Thought on Finances

The New Testament is full of warnings about a god closer to home, especially to today's believers: "You cannot serve both God and Money" (Luke 16:13).

Trying to do so is our downfall. What we tend to think of as prudent financial sense is often what the Old Testament believers thought of as prudent financial sense: playing both sides. Serving God and Money. Like those Israelites, we find people serving Money all around us. Our culture is permeated with it.

How do we know when we've made "making a living" more important than the living God? When we sacrifice freely of our time and energy at the altar of material gain. When we begin to feel safe because of our insurance policies, mutual funds, and level of income—rather than because God's hands are holding us. At that point we've lost contact with the mighty power of the living God.

The Israelites turned from the living God to a pile of carved wooden blocks. Are you a New Testament believer who's turning from the living God?

Edith Bajema

God's Words OF Life on

Forgiveness

In [Jesus] we have redemption through his blood, the forgiveness of sins, in accordance with the riches of God's grace.

Ephesians 1:7

You forgave the iniquity of your people[, LORD,]
and covered all their sins.

Psalm 85:2

You are forgiving and good, O Lord,
abounding in love to all who call to you.

Psalm 86:5

As far as the east is from the west,
so far has [God] removed our
transgressions from us.

Psalm 103:12

If anybody does sin, we have one who speaks to the Father in our defense—Jesus Christ, the Righteous One.

1 John 2:1

If we confess our sins, God is faithful and just and will forgive us our sins and purify us from all unrighteousness.

1 John 1:9

"I will forgive their wickedness
and will remember their sins no more,"
says the Lord.

Hebrews 8:12

Forgive as the LORD forgave you.

Colossians 3:13

Jesus said, "When you stand praying, if you hold anything against anyone, forgive him, so that your Father in heaven may forgive you your sins."

Mark 11:25

The Lord said, "I will cleanse [my people] from all the sin they have committed against me and will forgive all their sins of rebellion against me."

Jeremiah 33:8

Be kind and compassionate to one another, forgiving
each other, just as in Christ God forgave you.

Ephesians 4:32

"I, even I, am he who blots out
your transgressions, for my own sake,
and remembers your sins no more,"
says the Lord.

Isaiah 43:25

Blessed is he
whose transgressions are forgiven,
whose sins are covered.
Blessed is the man
whose sin the LORD does not count
against him
and in whose spirit is no deceit.

Psalm 32:1–2

"Come now, let us reason together,"
says the LORD.
"Though your sins are like scarlet,
they shall be as white as snow;
though they are red as crimson,
they shall be like wool."

Isaiah 1:18

Jesus said, "I tell you the truth, all the sins and blasphemies of men will be forgiven them."

Mark 3:28

Once you were alienated from God and were enemies in your minds because of your evil behavior. But now he has reconciled you by Christ's physical body through death to present you holy in God's sight, without blemish and free from accusation.

Colossians 1:21–22

You are forgiving and good, O Lord,
abounding in love to all who call to you.

Psalm 86:5

"If my people, who are called by my name, will humble themselves and pray and seek my face and turn from their wicked ways, then will I hear from heaven and will forgive their sin and will heal their land," says the Lord.

2 Chronicles 7:14

Devotional Thought on Forgiveness

Again and again our human nature wants to "teach people a lesson" or make things worse for them than they made it for us. We see revenge as a way of getting back, of making ourselves whole again. But it never works.

The solution Jesus offers is radical. There is no question of revenge or even bare restitution. He suggests simply that we become the shock absorbers of this world.

To receive a blow and to refuse to pass it on is an act that requires extraordinary generosity. For most people, it does not come naturally. We are too hard and resistant to be able to absorb the effect of an injury before we pass it on to a neighbor. We must become softer, gentler, more loving people, receiving a blow but unable by the fabric of our lives to transmit the force of it.

Love and forgiveness are the special vocations of the Christian, and when we exercise them we are able to find healing for our own wounds and offer balm for the healing of others.

Marcia Hollis

God's Words OF *Life on*

Friendship

A friend loves at all times.

Proverbs 17:17

Jesus said, "I no longer call you servants, because a servant does not know his master's business. Instead, I have called you friends, for everything that I learned from my Father I have made known to you."

John 15:15

*A man of many companions may come to ruin,
but there is a friend who
sticks closer than a brother.*

Proverbs 18:24

Jesus said, "Greater love has no one than this, that he lay down his life for his friends. You are my friends if you do what I command."

John 15:13–14

Perfume and incense bring joy to the heart,
and the pleasantness of one's friend springs
from his earnest counsel.

Proverbs 27:9

Two are better than one,
because they have a good return for their
work:
If one falls down,
his friend can help him up.
But pity the man who falls
and has no one to help him up!

Ecclesiastes 4:9–10

Devotional Thought on Friendship

As I think about friendship, I wonder if I had my life to live over, how differently I would live it.

Would I have invited more friends over for dinner, even if it were just for macaroni and cheese? Would I have sat on the lawn more often with my neighbors and visited while we watched the children play?

Would I have cried more often with them, and laughed more often when that was in order? Would I have said, "I'm sorry" more often?

I want to be more like this kind of friend:

F — Fun-loving; Faithful
R — Risk being Real, even misunderstood
I — Interested in the welfare of others
E — Expect the best of others; Empathetic
N — Natural relationship; Nonexclusive
D — Diplomatic; Delightful; Durable
S — Sympathetic; Supportive; Stable
H — Helpful; Hopeful; Happy
I — Interdependent by helping others
P — Patient; Protective of confidences; Personable

If I were given another opportunity at life and friendship, I would seize every minute of it . . . and live it for Jesus.

Doris W. Greig

God's Words OF Life on

Frustration

"Call to me and I will answer you and tell you great and unsearchable things you do not know," says the Lord.

Jeremiah 33:3

"I will make an everlasting covenant with [my people]: I will never stop doing good to them, and I will inspire them to fear me, so that they will never turn away from me," says the Lord.

Jeremiah 32:40

If God is for us, who can be against us? He who did not spare his own Son, but gave him up for us all—how will he not also, along with him, graciously give us all things?

Romans 8:31–32

God is faithful; he will not let you be tempted beyond what you can bear. But when you are tempted, he will also provide a way out so that you can stand up under it.

1 Corinthians 10:13

A righteous man may have many troubles,
but the LORD delivers him
from them all.

Psalm 34:19

Let us hold unswervingly to the hope we profess, for [God] who promised is faithful.

Hebrews 10:23

Let us acknowledge the LORD;
let us press on to acknowledge him.
As surely as the sun rises,
he will appear;
he will come to us like the winter rains,
like the spring rains that water the earth.

Hosea 6:3

We know that in all things God works for the good of those who love him, who have been called according to his purpose.

Romans 8:28

"So do not fear, for I am with you;
      do not be dismayed, for I am your God.
I will strengthen you and help you;
      I will uphold you with my
            righteous right hand."

                                                Isaiah 41:10

Though I walk in the midst of trouble,
      you preserve my life;
you stretch out your hand
            against the anger of my foes,
      with your right hand you save me.
The LORD will fulfill [his purpose] for me;
      your love, O LORD, endures forever—
      do not abandon the works of
      your hands.

                                                Psalm 138:7–8

Cast your cares on the LORD
      and he will sustain you;
he will never let the righteous fall.

                                                Psalm 55:22

Since we are surrounded by such a great cloud of witnesses, let us throw off everything that hinders and the sin that so easily entangles, and let us run with perseverance the race marked out for us. Let us fix our eyes on Jesus, the author and perfecter of our faith, who for the joy set before him endured the cross, scorning its shame, and sat down at the right hand of the throne of God. Consider him who endured such opposition from sinful men, so that you will not grow weary and lose heart.

Hebrews 12:1–3

All a man's ways seem right to him,
but the LORD weighs the heart.
To do what is right and just
is more acceptable to the LORD than sacrifice.
Proverbs 21:2–3

As you know, we consider blessed those who have persevered. You have heard of Job's perseverance and have seen what the Lord finally brought about.

James 5:11

The Lord says, "Have I not commanded you? Be strong and courageous. Do not be terrified; do not be discouraged, for the Lord your God will be with you wherever you go."

Joshua 1:9

Devotional Thought on Frustration

There is only one way to eat an elephant: a bite at a time. Maybe you know that already. I didn't—until Beverly Johnson told the world after she, the first woman to do so alone, reached the top of thirty-six-hundred-feet-high El Capitan in Yosemite National Park, California.

"That's what I kept saying, 'A bite at a time, a bite at a time . . . ,'" the smiling Beverly said of her ten-day struggle up the gigantic granite mass that rises unbroken from the Yosemite Valley.

We can all "eat elephants" by Beverly's formula, can't we? It makes little difference whether it's all the things we have to accomplish, a test we have to take, a physical condition we have to live with, a broken heart that needs healing. Her reasoning works.

Haven't you often wished that you could magically leave your problems? Most of us feel that way, but the world doesn't stop for us to get off. We dig in with whatever equipment we have; we work our way up slowly; and, remember this: We have the solid Rock to lean upon! God is always there.

June Masters Bacher

God's Presence

Keep your lives free from the love of money and be content with what you have, because God has said,
> "Never will I leave you;
> never will I forsake you."

Hebrews 13:5

Jesus said, "Surely I am with you always, to the very end of the age."

Matthew 28:20

For the sake of his great name the LORD will not reject his people, because the LORD was pleased to make you his own.

1 Samuel 12:22

"Do not fear, for I am with you;
    do not be dismayed, for I am your God.
I will strengthen you and help you;
    I will uphold you with my righteous right
        hand."

Isaiah 41:10

Who shall separate us from the love of Christ? Shall trouble or hardship or persecution or famine or naked-ness or danger or sword? . . . No, in all these things we are more than conquerors through him who loved us. For I am convinced that neither death nor life, neither angels nor demons, neither the present nor the future, nor any powers, neither height nor depth, nor anything else in all creation, will be able to separate us from the love of God that is in Christ Jesus our Lord.

Romans 8:35, 37–39

"Be still, and know that I am God."

Psalm 46:10

The eternal God is your refuge,
    and underneath are the everlasting arms.

Deuteronomy 33:27

The LORD your God is a merciful God; he will not abandon or destroy you or forget the covenant with your forefathers.

Deuteronomy 4:31

Be strong and courageous. Do not be afraid or terrified . . . for the LORD your God goes with you; he will never leave you nor forsake you.

Deuteronomy 31:6

Though my father and mother forsake me,
the LORD will receive me.

Psalm 27:10

"Though the mountains be shaken
and the hills be removed,
yet my unfailing love for you will not be shaken
nor my covenant of peace be removed,"
says the LORD, who has compassion on you.

Isaiah 54:10

God is our refuge and strength,
an ever-present help in trouble.

Psalm 46:1

Jesus said, "Remain in me, and I will remain in you."

John 15:4

Jesus said, "Here I am! I stand at the door and knock. If anyone hears my voice and opens the door, I will come in and eat with him, and he with me."

Revelation 3:20

Come near to God and he will come near to you.

James 4:8

Those who know your name will trust in you,
for you, LORD, have never forsaken those
who seek you.

Psalm 9:10

"[The one who trusts in me] will call upon me,
and I will answer him;
I will be with him in trouble,
I will deliver him and honor him.
With long life will I satisfy him
and show him my salvation,"
says the Lord.

Psalm 91:15–16

"See, I have engraved you on the palms of my
hands;
your walls are ever before me,"
says the Lord.

Isaiah 49:16

"You will seek me and find me when you seek me with all your heart," says the Lord.

Jeremiah 29:13

Where can I go from your Spirit?
Where can I flee from your presence?
If I go up to the heavens, you are there;
if I make my bed in the depths, you are
there.
If I rise on the wings of the dawn,
if I settle on the far side of the sea,
even there your hand will guide me,
your right hand will hold me fast.

Psalm 139:7–10

How great is your goodness[, LORD,]
which you have stored up for those who
fear you,
which you bestow in the sight of men
on those who take refuge in you.
In the shelter of your presence you hide them
from the intrigues of men;
in your dwelling you keep them safe
from accusing tongues.

Psalm 31:19–20

The eyes of the LORD are on the righteous
> *and his ears are attentive to their cry. . . .*
The righteous cry out, and the LORD hears
> *them;*
>> *he delivers them from all their troubles.*
>>> Psalm 34:15, 17

The LORD is my shepherd, I shall not be in
> *want.*
>> *He makes me lie down in*
>>> *green pastures,*
he leads me beside quiet waters,
> *he restores my soul.*
He guides me in paths of righteousness
> *for his name's sake.*
Even thought I walk
> *through the valley of the shadow of death*
I will fear no evil,
> *for you are with me;*
your rod and your staff,
> *they comfort me.*
You prepare a table before me
> *in the presence of my enemies.*
You anoint my head with oil;
> *my cup overflows,*

Surely goodness and love will
follow me
all the days of my life,
and I will dwell in the house of the LORD
forever.

Psalm 23

Devotional Thought on God's Presence

Boredom can rob a person of *joy*. Apathy may not sink my boat but it can becalm me and cause despair as the wind is taken out of the sails of my life. I thought about two verses in Proverbs. "I was filled with delight day after day, rejoicing always in his presence, rejoicing in his whole world and delighting in mankind" (Proverbs 8:30–31).

Because Christ lives in us, we can be filled with delight day after day. And those things that can and will delight us have nothing to do with position or ministry. We can have delight in the dull, monotonous months, in the routine, mundane days, in the lean, hungry years.

I'll probably have to remind myself often when dullness of soul creeps over me, but the truth is that God provides . . . *no excuse for boredom*.

Carole Mayhall

God's Words OF Life on

Grace

There is now no condemnation for those who are in Christ Jesus.

Romans 8:1

[God] does not treat us as our sins deserve
*   or repay us according to our iniquities.*
For as high as the heavens are above the earth,
*   so great is his love for those who fear him;*
as far as the east is from the west,
*   so far has he removed our transgressions*
*   from us.*

Psalm 103:10–12

Jesus said, "God did not send his Son into the world to condemn the world, but to save the world through him."

John 3:17

If anyone is in Christ, he is a new creation; the old has gone, the new has come!

2 Corinthians 5:17

Jesus said, "I tell you the truth, whoever hears my word and believes him who sent me has eternal life and will not be condemned."

John 5:24

Grace, mercy and peace from God the Father and from Jesus Christ, the Father's Son, will be with us in truth and love.

2 John 1:3

Let the wicked forsake his way
and the evil man his thoughts.
Let him turn to the LORD, and
he will have mercy on him,
and to our God, for he will freely pardon.

Isaiah 55:7

For you know the grace of our Lord Jesus Christ, that though he was rich, yet for your sakes he became poor, so that you through his poverty might become rich.

2 Corinthians 8:9

But God demonstrates his own love for us in this: While we were still sinners, Christ died for us.

Romans 5:8

But when the kindness and love of God our Savior appeared, he saved us, not because of righteous things we had done, but because of his mercy. He saved us through the washing of rebirth and renewal by the Holy Spirit, whom he poured out on us generously through Jesus Christ our Savior, so that, having been justified by his grace, we might become heirs having the hope of eternal life.

Titus 3:4–7

When you were dead in your sins, . . . God made you alive with Christ. He forgave us all our sins, having canceled the written code, with its regulations, that was against us and that stood opposed to us; he took it away, nailing it to the cross.

Colossians 2:13–14

You are a forgiving God, gracious and compassionate, slow to anger and abounding in love.

Nehemiah 9:17

The Lord your God is gracious and compassionate. He will not turn his face from you if you return to him.

2 Chronicles 30:9

The wages of sin is death, but the gift of God is eternal life in Christ Jesus our Lord.

Romans 6:23

For we do not have a high priest who is unable to sympathize with our weaknesses, but we have one who has been tempted in every way, just as we are—yet was without sin. Let us then approach the throne of grace with confidence, so that we may receive mercy and find grace to help us in our time of need.

Hebrews 4:15–16

Because of his great love for us, God, who is rich in mercy, made us alive with Christ even when we were dead in transgressions—it is by grace you have been saved. And God raised us up with Christ and seated us with him in the heavenly realms in Christ Jesus, in order that in the coming ages he might show the incomparable riches of his grace, expressed in his kindness to us in Christ Jesus. For it is by grace you have been saved, through faith—and this not from yourselves, it is the gift of God—not by works, so that no one can boast.

Ephesians 2:4–9

[The LORD] mocks proud mockers
but gives grace to the humble.

Proverbs 3:34

From the fullness of his grace we have all received one blessing after another. For the law was given through Moses; grace and truth came through Jesus Christ. No one has ever seen God, but God the One and Only, who is at the Father's side, has made him known.

John 1:16–18

All have sinned and fall short of the glory of God, and are justified freely by his grace through the redemption that came by Christ Jesus.

Romans 3:23–24

God is able to make all grace abound to you, so that in all things at all times, having all that you need, you will abound in every good work.

2 Corinthians 9:8

Jesus said, "My grace is sufficient for you, for my power is made perfect in weakness."

2 Corinthians 12:9

Grace and peace be yours in abundance through the knowledge of God and of Jesus our Lord. His divine power has given us everything we need for life and godliness through our knowledge of him who called us by his own glory and goodness.

2 Peter 1:2–3

Devotional Thought on Grace

"Guilty!" cries the crowd, and they take up stones. The woman has no defender. Caught in the act, dragged naked out of the bedroom, a cloak thrown quickly around her shoulders to keep out the cold. But it cannot hide her sin. Picture yourself as that woman—humiliated, terrified.

You are thrust in front of your neighbors, townspeople, people you know. You feel so ashamed. You want to run and hide, but where can you go?

Even your own heart condemns you. "Guilty!" A sharp stab of pain cuts at the core of who you are. Overwhelmed by waves of sadness and shame, you sink to the ground, huddled in a heap.

Then Jesus speaks to the crowd with a voice sure and steady. There is silence. A long silence. Now *their* heads are bowed. *Thud.* A hard rock hits the ground. *Thud.* Another, then another. One by one your accusers walk away.

You are left alone with Jesus. Quietly, he comes close. He smiles and helps you to your feet. "Go now," he says, "and leave your life of sin" (John 8:11).

Betsy Lee

God's Words OF Life on

Grief and Death

Multitudes who sleep in the dust of the earth will awake: some to everlasting life. . . . Those who are wise will shine like the brightness of the heavens, and those who lead many to righteousness, like the stars for ever and ever.

Daniel 12:2–3

If only for this life we have hope in Christ, we are to be pitied more than all men. But Christ has indeed been raised from the dead, the firstfruits of those who have fallen asleep. For since death came through a man, the resurrection of the dead comes also through a man. For as in Adam all die, so in Christ all will be made alive.

1 Corinthians 15:19–22

Listen, I tell you a mystery: We will not all sleep, but we will all be changed—in a flash, in the twinkling of an eye, at the last trumpet. For the trumpet will sound, the dead will be raised imperishable, and we will be changed. For the perishable must clothe itself with the imperishable, and the mortal with immortality. When the perishable has been clothed with the imperishable, and the mortal with immortality, then the saying that is written will come true: "Death has been swallowed up in victory."

"Where, O death, is your victory?
Where, O death, is your sting?"
1 Corinthians 15:51–55

We believe that Jesus died and rose again and so we believe that God will bring with Jesus those who have fallen asleep in him. According to the Lord's own word, we tell you that we who are still alive, who are left till the coming of the Lord, will certainly not precede those who have fallen asleep. For the Lord himself will come down from heaven, with a loud command, with the voice of the archangel and with the trumpet call of God, and the dead in Christ will rise first. After that, we who are still alive and are left will be caught up together with them in the clouds to meet the Lord in the air. And so we will be with the Lord forever.

1 Thessalonians 4:14–17

I heard a loud voice from the throne saying, "Now the dwelling of God is with men, and he will live with them. They will be his people, and God himself will be with them and be their God. He will wipe every tear from their eyes. There will be no more death or mourning or crying or pain, for the old order of things has passed away."

Revelation 21:3–4

Even though I walk
    through the valley of the shadow of death,
I will fear no evil,
    for you are with me;
your rod and your staff,
    they comfort me.

Psalm 23:4

Into your hands I commit my spirit;
    redeem me, O LORD, the God of truth.

Psalm 31:5

None of us lives to himself alone and none of us dies to himself alone. If we live, we live to the Lord; and if we die, we die to the Lord. So, whether we live or die, we belong to the Lord.

Romans 14:7–8

You guide me with your counsel,
    and afterward you will take me into glory.
Whom have I in heaven but you?
    And earth has nothing I desire besides you.
My flesh and my heart may fail,
    but God is the strength of my heart
    and my portion forever.

Psalm 73:24–26

Precious in the sight of the LORD
    is the death of his saints.

Psalm 116:15

Those who walk uprightly
    enter into peace;
    they find rest as they lie in death.

Isaiah 57:2

We know that if the earthly tent we live in is destroyed, we have a building from God, an eternal house in heaven, not built by human hands.

2 Corinthians 5:1

We are confident, I say, and would prefer to be away from the body and at home with the Lord.

2 Corinthians 5:8

To live is Christ and to die is gain.

Philippians 1:21

Jesus died for us so that, whether we are awake or asleep, we may live together with him.

1 Thessalonians 5:10

There is in store for me the crown of righteousness, which the Lord, the righteous Judge, will award to me on that day—and not only to me, but also to all who have longed for his appearing.

2 Timothy 4:8

Since the children have flesh and blood, [Christ] too shared in their humanity so that by his death he might destroy him who holds the power of death—that is, the devil—and free those who all their lives were held in slavery by their fear of death.

Hebrews 2:14–15

I heard a voice from heaven say, "Write: Blessed are the dead who die in the Lord from now on."

"Yes," says the Spirit, "they will rest from their labor, for their deeds will follow them."

Revelation 14:13

Jesus said, "Blessed are those who mourn,
for they will be comforted."

Matthew 5:4

If Christ is in you, your body is dead because of sin, yet your spirit is alive because of righteousness. And if the Spirit of him who raised Jesus from the dead is living in you, he who raised Christ from the dead will also give life to your mortal bodies through his Spirit, who lives in you.

Romans 8:10–11

We who have fled to take hold of the hope offered to us may be greatly encouraged. We have this hope as an anchor for the soul, firm and secure.

Hebrews 6:18–19

Devotional Thought on Grief and Death

In the face of death there was no one to blame, no sign, no job, no certainty, no cure in sight, and no telling what God had in mind. I was alone with God, wholly in his determined, unpredictable will.

These days were filled with the peculiar and strangling frenzy of waiting. I cried a lot, worried a lot, questioned a lot, felt lost, slept little, and beyond all of that, God began to touch me deeply.

I started being honest, dreadfully honest.

I didn't like the idea of death. Death is, for me, the great intruder. I was angry with God that he would ask me even to consider it. I had questions for which I didn't think God had the answers, or if he did, he wasn't willing to share them with me. And when I asked those questions, a surprising thing happened: what was meant as confrontation became release.

Far from resenting my questions, God welcomed them. He comprehended my pain and translated my helplessness into certain strength.

I don't know how. I don't know much about such grace. God gave no answers then, just his presence. Just that. And his grace was sufficient.

Deforia Lane

God's Words OF Life on

Guidance

If any of you lacks wisdom, he should ask God, who gives generously to all without finding fault, and it will be given to him.

James 1:5

"I will instruct you and teach you in the way you should go;
I will counsel you and watch over you,"
says the Lord.

Psalm 32:8

Your word[, O LORD,] is a lamp to my feet
and a light for my path.

Psalm 119:105

When you walk, they will guide you;
    when you sleep, they will watch over you;
    when you awake, they will speak to you.
For these commands are a lamp,
    this teaching is a light,
and the corrections of discipline
    are the way to life.

Proverbs 6:22–23

The Lord says, "Do not let this Book of the Law depart from your mouth; meditate on it day and night, so that you may be careful to do everything written in it. Then you will be prosperous and successful."

Joshua 1:8

Commit to the LORD whatever you do,
    and your plans will succeed.

Proverbs 16:3

If the LORD delights in a man's way,
    he makes his steps firm;
though he stumble, he will not fall,
    for the LORD upholds him with his hand.

Psalm 37:23–24

[O LORD,] since you are my rock and my fortress,
    for the sake of your name lead and guide me.

Psalm 31:3

Trust in the LORD with all your heart
and lean not on your own understanding;
in all your ways acknowledge him,
and he will make your paths straight.

Proverbs 3:5–6

This is what the LORD says—
your Redeemer, the Holy One of Israel:
"I am the LORD your God,
who teaches you what is best for you,
who directs you in the way you should go."

Isaiah 48:17

The LORD will guide you always;
he will satisfy your needs in a sun-
scorched land
and will strengthen your frame.
You will be like a well-watered garden,
like a spring whose waters never fail.

Isaiah 58:11

Jesus said, "When he, the Spirit of truth, comes, he will guide you into all truth. He will not speak on his own; he will speak only what he hears, and he will tell you what is yet to come."

John 16:13

The way of a fool seems right to him,
but a wise man listens to advice.

Proverbs 12:15

Your commands make me wiser than my enemies,
for they are ever with me[, O LORD.]

Psalm 119:98

Show me your ways, O LORD,
teach me your paths;
guide me in your truth and teach me,
for you are God my Savior,
and my hope is in you all day long.

Psalm 25:4–5

We know that in all things God works for the good of those who love him, who have been called according to his purpose.

Romans 8:28

You discern my going out and my lying down;
you are familiar with all my ways[, O LORD].

Psalm 139:3

The LORD will fulfill his purpose for me;
your love, O LORD, endures forever—
do not abandon the works of your hands.

Psalm 138:8

Let us acknowledge the LORD;
let us press on to acknowledge him.
As surely as the sun rises,
he will appear;
he will come to us like the winter rains,
like the spring rains that water the earth.

Hosea 6:3

Jesus replied, "If anyone loves me, he will obey my teaching. My Father will love him, and we will come to him and make our home with him. He who does not love me will not obey my teaching. These words you hear are not my own; they belong to the Father who sent me."

John 14:23–24

The LORD gives wisdom,
and from his mouth come knowledge
and understanding.

Proverbs 2:6

"I know the plans I have for you," declares the LORD, "plans to prosper you and not to harm you, plans to give you hope and a future."

Jeremiah 29:11

Pay attention and listen to the sayings of the wise;
apply your heart to what I teach,

for it is pleasing when you keep them in your
        heart
    and have all of them ready on your lips.
So that your trust may be in the LORD.
                            Proverbs 22:17–19

In your unfailing love you will lead
    the people you have redeemed[, O LORD].
In your strength you will guide them
    to your holy dwelling.
                            Exodus 15:13

Guide me in your truth and teach me,
    for you are God my Savior,
    and my hope is in you all day long.
                            Psalm 25:5

I guide you in the way of wisdom
    and lead you along straight paths.
                            Proverbs 4:11

This God is our God for ever and ever;
    he will be our guide even to the end.
                            Psalm 48:14

Devotional Thought on Guidance

Everybody should have a friend like Ralph. He can fix a lamp or a lawn mower, refinish furniture, build bookshelves. All by himself he has transformed his garage into a workshop and completely remodeled his mother's house.

One day, marveling at these results over coffee, I asked, "Ralph, where did you learn to do all this?"

Thoughtfully he sipped his coffee, his blue eyes twinkling. Then Ralph gave me the words of his own special prayer:

> Jesus stand beside me.
> Guide and direct my life.
> Teach me what I need to know.
> Help me with my work.
> Let me serve you and others,
> That I may be worthy of God's grace.

Ralph's special prayer has become a part of my own life now. I say it every morning. And all day. Whenever I am anxious or confused about a situation, one phrase comes to my rescue: "Teach me what I need to know." Of all the things Ralph has done to help me, his prayer has helped most of all.

Marjorie Holmes

God's Words
OF Life on

Holiness

It is the LORD your God you must follow, and him you must revere. Keep his commands and obey him; serve him and hold fast to him.

Deuteronomy 13:4

I urge you, brothers, in view of God's mercy, to offer your bodies as living sacrifices, holy and pleasing to God—this is your spiritual act of worship. Do not conform any longer to the pattern of this world, but be transformed by the renewing of your mind. Then you will be able to test and approve what God's will is—his good, pleasing and perfect will.

Romans 12:1–2

Make every effort to live in peace with all men and to be holy; without holiness no one will see the Lord.

Hebrews 12:14

God did not call us to be impure, but to live a holy life.

1 Thessalonians 4:7

[God] chose us in him before the creation of the world to be holy and blameless in his sight.

Ephesians 1:4

We have been made holy through the sacrifice of the body of Jesus Christ once for all.

Hebrews 10:10

*Does the LORD delight in burnt offerings
        and sacrifices
    as much as in obeying the voice of the
        LORD?
To obey is better than sacrifice,
    and to heed is better than the fat of rams.*

1 Samuel 15:22

"Obey me, and I will be your God and you will be my people. Walk in all the ways I command you, that it may go well with you."

Jeremiah 7:23

Be very careful to keep the commandment and the law . . . to love the LORD your God, to walk in all his ways, to obey his commands, to hold fast to him and to serve him with all your heart and all your soul.

Joshua 22:5

"Consecrate yourselves and be holy, because I am the LORD your God. Keep my decrees and follow them. I am the LORD, who makes you holy."

Leviticus 20:7–8

Now that you have been set free from sin and have become slaves to God, the benefit you reap leads to holiness, and the result is eternal life.

Romans 6:22

God has said: "I will live with them and walk among them, and I will be their God, and they will be my people." . . . Since we have these promises, dear friends, let us purify ourselves from everything that contaminates body and spirit, perfecting holiness out of reverence for God.

2 Corinthians 6:16, 7:1

May [the Lord] strengthen your hearts so that you will be blameless and holy in the presence of our God and Father when our Lord Jesus comes with all his holy ones.

1 Thessalonians 3:13

[God's] divine power has given us everything we need for life and godliness through our knowledge of him who called us by his own glory and goodness.

2 Peter 1:3

Whatever is true, whatever is noble, whatever is right, whatever is pure, whatever is lovely, whatever is admirable—if anything is excellent or praiseworthy—think about such things.

Philippians 4:8

Who among the gods is like you, O LORD?
Who is like you—
majestic in holiness,
awesome in glory,
working wonders?
You stretched out your right hand
and the earth swallowed them.
In your unfailing love you will lead
the people you have redeemed.
In your strength you will guide them
to your holy dwelling.

Exodus 15:11–13

Ascribe to the LORD the glory due his name.
Bring an offering and come before him;
worship the LORD in the splendor of his holiness.

1 Chronicles 16:29

You were taught, with regard to your former way of life, to put off your old self, which is being corrupted by its deceitful desires; to be made new in the attitude of your minds; and to put on the new self, created to be like God in true righteousness and holiness.

Ephesians 4:22–24

Just as he who called you is holy, so be holy in all you do; for it is written: "Be holy, because I am holy."

1 Peter 1:15–16

It is because of him that you are in Christ Jesus, who has become for us wisdom from God—that is, our righteousness, holiness and redemption. Therefore, as it is written: "Let him who boasts boast in the Lord."

1 Corinthians 1:30–31

Devotional Thought on Holiness

DO—Do not worry over things that may never happen, and even if they happen, worry will not help.

RE—Radiate good will and a spirit of benevolence. Like laughter, it makes you feel better.

ME—Mete kindness, understanding, tolerance, and forgiveness generously.

FA—Far-reaching are the therapeutic benefits of spiritual thinking. Resentment, hatred, and envy pack radioactive fallout that gnaws at your vitals. They are self-consuming.

SO—Sow the seeds of love, friendship, empathy, and helpfulness. These hardy seeds take root in the crustiest ground.

LA—Laugh at yourself now and then. You who can laugh at yourself are less apt to be at war with yourself.

TI—Teach yourself awareness and appreciation of all the wonders of nature. Thank God daily for the precious gift of life. Genuine gratitude and discontent are never found together.

DO—Do not expect someone else to open the door to happiness for you. You must do it yourself. You alone have the key. Turn it.

Author Unknown

God's Words
OF Life on

Honesty

A truthful witness gives honest testimony,
but a false witness tells lies.
Proverbs 12:17

Show me your ways, O LORD,
teach me your paths;
guide me in your truth and teach me,
for you are God my Savior,
and my hope is in you all day long.
Psalm 25:4–5

The LORD is near to all who call on him,
to all who call on him in truth.
Psalm 145:18

Kings take pleasure in honest lips;
   they value a man who speaks the truth.

Proverbs 16:13

"These are the things you are to do: Speak the truth to each other, and render true and sound judgment in your courts," declares the Lord.

Zechariah 8:16

He who walks righteously
   and speaks what is right,
who rejects gain from extortion
   and keeps his hand from accepting bribes,
who stops his ears against plots of murder
   and shuts his eyes against contemplating evil—
this is the man who will dwell on the heights.

Isaiah 33:15–16

In everything set them an example by doing what is good. In your teaching show integrity, seriousness and soundness of speech that cannot be condemned, so that those who oppose you may be ashamed because they have nothing bad to say about us.

Titus 2:7–8

I strive always to keep my conscience clear before God and man.

Acts 24:16

Whatever is true, whatever is noble, whatever is right, whatever is pure, whatever is lovely, whatever is admirable—if anything is excellent or praiseworthy—think about such things.

Philippians 4:8

Do not withhold your mercy from me, O LORD;
may your love and your truth always
protect me.

Psalm 40:11

Obey your earthly masters in everything; and do it, not only when their eye is on you and to win their favor, but with sincerity of heart and reverence for the Lord. Whatever you do, work at it with all your heart, as working for the Lord, not for men.

Colossians 3:22–23

Live such good lives among the pagans that, though they accuse you of doing wrong, they may see your good deeds and glorify God on the day he visits us.

1 Peter 2:12

Judge me, O LORD, according to my righteousness,
according to my integrity, O Most High.

Psalm 7:8

LORD, *who may dwell in your sanctuary?*
　　Who may live on your holy hill?
He whose walk is blameless
　　and who does what is righteous,
who speaks the truth from his heart.

Psalm 15:1–2

The man of integrity walks securely,
　　but he who takes crooked paths will be
　　　　found out.

Proverbs 10:9

He has showed you, O man, what is good.
　　And what does the LORD require of you?
To act justly and to love mercy
　　and to walk humbly with your God.

Micah 6:8

Jesus said, "Whoever can be trusted with very little can also be trusted with much, and whoever is dishonest with very little will also be dishonest with much."

Luke 16:10

Devotional Thought on Honesty

Last spring, my husband and I had our income tax returns done. I was extremely busy with all of the usual activities of life at the time, and hurriedly ran about pulling open drawers, looking for records and receipts, all about an hour before I was supposed to have the information gathered together. I *guesstimated* how much we had donated for charities and how much we had spent for medical expenses. I began to feel uncomfortable, but silently reasoned that I had done all I was able to do under the circumstances.

The next morning, as I left the house for my Bible study, I murmured a quick prayer. "Lord . . . If you want me to go back through all my records and do it right, I will. Just let me know." On the way to the Bible study, the woman who was driving began to talk about . . . being obedient to the Lord even in small things. She said her mother laughs at her for being so honest on her income tax! I squirmed in my seat. I knew what I had to do. Although it was slightly embarrassing to call our accountant back with the correct figures, I felt better once I had. And I felt a whole lot better knowing that I had been obedient to the Lord's voice.

Nicole Hill

God's Words OF Life on

Hope

Be strong and take heart,
*   all you who hope in the LORD.*
*   Psalm 31:24*

The eyes of the LORD are on those who fear him,
*   on those whose hope is in his unfailing love.*
*   Psalm 33:18*

May your unfailing love rest upon us, O LORD,
*   even as we put our hope in you.*
*   Psalm 33:22*

I wait for you, O LORD;
*   you will answer, O Lord my God.*
*   Psalm 38:15*

Those who hope in the LORD
will renew their strength.
They will soar on wings like eagles;
they will run and not grow weary,
they will walk and not be faint.

Isaiah 40:31

Why are you downcast, O my soul?
Why so disturbed within me?
Put your hope in God,
for I will yet praise him,
my Savior and my God.

Psalm 43:5

You have been my hope, O Sovereign LORD,
my confidence since my youth.

Psalm 71:5

Now to him who is able to do immeasurably more than all
we ask or imagine, according to his power that is at work
within us, to him be glory in the church and in Christ
Jesus throughout all generations for ever and ever! Amen.

Ephesians 3:20–21

May those who fear [God] rejoice when they see me,
for I have put my hope in your word.

Psalm 119:74

Sustain me according to your promise, and I
     will live;
     do not let my hopes be dashed.
                              Psalm 119:116

Put your hope in the LORD,
     for with the LORD is unfailing love
     and with him is full redemption.
                              Psalm 130:7

Blessed is he whose help is the God of Jacob,
     whose hope is in the LORD his God,
the Maker of heaven and earth,
     the sea, and everything in them—
the LORD, who remains faithful forever.
                              Psalm 146:5–6

Hope deferred makes the heart sick,
     but a longing fulfilled is a tree of life.
                              Proverbs 13:12

Blessed is the man who trusts in the LORD,
     whose confidence is in him.
He will be like a tree planted by the water
     that sends out its roots by the stream.
It does not fear when heat comes;
     its leaves are always green.

It has no worries in a year of drought
and never fails to bear fruit.

Jeremiah 17:7–8

Yet this I call to mind
and therefore I have hope:
Because of the LORD's great love we are not
consumed,
for his compassions never fail.

Lamentations 3:21–22

I say to myself, "The LORD is my portion;
therefore I will wait for him."
The LORD is good to those whose hope is in him,
to the one who seeks him.

Lamentations 3:24–25

We also rejoice in our sufferings, because we know that suffering produces perseverance; perseverance, character; and character, hope. And hope does not disappoint us, because God has poured out his love into our hearts by the Holy Spirit, whom he has given us.

Romans 5:3–5

Everything that was written in the past was written to teach us, so that through endurance and the encouragement of the Scriptures we might have hope.

Romans 15:4

May the God of hope fill you with all joy and peace as you trust in him, so that you may overflow with hope by the power of the Holy Spirit.

Romans 15:13

We continually remember before our God and Father your work produced by faith, your labor prompted by love, and your endurance inspired by hope in our Lord Jesus Christ.

1 Thessalonians 1:3

May our Lord Jesus Christ himself and God our Father, who loved us and by his grace gave us eternal encouragement and good hope, encourage your hearts and strengthen you in every good deed and word.

2 Thessalonians 2:16–17

I am convinced that neither death nor life, neither angels nor demons, neither the present nor the future, nor any powers, neither height nor depth, nor anything else in all creation, will be able to separate us from the love of God that is in Christ Jesus our Lord.

Romans 8:38–39

Faith is being sure of what we hope for and certain of what we do not see.

Hebrews 11:1

In your hearts set apart Christ as Lord. Always be prepared to give an answer to everyone who asks you to give the reason for the hope that you have.

1 Peter 3:15

Be joyful in hope.

Romans 12:12

The LORD is my helper;
I will not be afraid. . . .
Jesus Christ is the same yesterday and today
and forever.

Hebrews 13:6, 8

Know also that wisdom is sweet to your soul;
if you find it, there is a future hope for you,
and your hope will not be cut off.

Proverbs 24:14

Devotional Thought on Hope

In the Russian prison where Solzhenitsyn was, no one was allowed to speak. There was nothing to read, and no encouragement of any kind to sustain life. He knew that if he tried to escape he would be shot, but he thought, *At least, that will be the end of that!*

When a break in the work day came, he sat under a tree. Just then a shadow came across the grass. He looked up into the eyes of the new man who had recently come as a prisoner and saw something he had never seen in any face in prison before—a message of love and concern.

As their eyes locked in silence, the prisoner took a step forward and drew a cross on the ground with a stick. Solzhenitsyn said new hope surged within him at that moment. *Jesus does love me. He is in command. It is not hopeless!* Three days later he was released from that prison. He knew with powerful certainty that God is sovereign and there is still hope.

We mustn't give up! We might be the one to communicate hope to someone else, maybe by a gesture, maybe without words. We must love and pray and hold one another up.

Mary C. Crowley

God's Words
OF Life on

Hospitality

"Is this not the kind of fasting I have cho-
     sen: . . .
Is it not to share your food with the hungry
     and to provide the poor wanderer with
          shelter—
when you see the naked, to clothe him,
     and not to turn away from your own
          flesh and blood?
Then your light will break forth like the dawn,
     and your healing will quickly appear;
then your righteousness will go before you,
     and the glory of the LORD
          will be your rear guard," says the Lord.
                              Isaiah 58:6–8

Jesus said, "I was hungry and you gave me something to eat, I was thirsty and you gave me something to drink, I was a stranger and you invited me in, I needed clothes and you clothed me, I was sick and you looked after me, I was in prison and you came to visit me. Then the righteous will answer him, 'Lord, when did we see you hungry and feed you, or thirsty and give you something to drink? When did we see you a stranger and invite you in, or needing clothes and clothe you? When did we see you sick or in prison and go to visit you?' . . . I tell you the truth, whatever you did for one of the least of these brothers of mine, you did for me."

Matthew 25:35–40

Make every effort to add to your faith goodness; and to goodness, knowledge; and to knowledge, self-control; and to self-control, perseverance; and to perseverance, godliness; and to godliness, brotherly kindness; and to brotherly kindness, love. For if you possess these qualities in increasing measure, they will keep you from being ineffective and unproductive in your knowledge of our Lord Jesus Christ.

2 Peter 1:5–8

Then Jesus said to his host, "When you give a luncheon or dinner, do not invite your friends, your brothers or relatives, or your rich neighbors; if you do, they may invite you back and so you will be repaid. But when you give a banquet, invite the poor, the crippled, the lame, the blind, and you will be blessed. Although they cannot repay you, you will be repaid at the resurrection of the righteous."

Luke 14:12–14

Share with God's people who are in need. Practice hospitality.

Romans 12:13

Do not forget to entertain strangers, for by so doing some people have entertained angels without knowing it.

Hebrews 13:2

This service that you perform is not only supplying the needs of God's people but is also overflowing in many expressions of thanks to God. Because of the service by which you have proved yourselves, men will praise God for the obedience that accompanies your confession of the gospel of Christ, and for your generosity in sharing with them and with everyone else.

2 Corinthians 9:12–13

Offer hospitality to one another without grumbling.

1 Peter 4:9

If anyone speaks, he should do it as one speaking the very words of God. If anyone serves, he should do it with the strength God provides, so that in all things God may be praised through Jesus Christ. To him be the glory and the power for ever and ever. Amen.

1 Peter 4:11

Do not forget to do good and to share with others, for with such sacrifices God is pleased.

Hebrews 13:16

When an alien lives with you in your land, do not mistreat him. The alien living with you must be treated as one of your native-born. Love him as yourself.

Leviticus 19:33–34

Devotional Thought on Hospitality

The essence of hospitality is a heart open to God, with room prepared for the guest of the Holy Spirit, which welcomes the presence of Christ. This is what we share with those to whom we open our doors. We give to them Christ and think nothing of what we give of ourselves.

My three-dollar oak table has become an altar where hungry hearts have been nourished with the bread of life. Our living room has been made a sanctuary where sacraments of comfort and communion have been offered, where we have shared in the fellowship of human suffering and human delight.

If Christians, corporately, would begin to practice hospitality, we could play significant roles in redeeming our society. There is no better place to be about the redemption of society than in the Christian servant's home; and the more we deal with the captive, the blind, the downtrodden, the more we realize that in this inhospitable world, a Christian home is a miracle to be shared.

Karen Burton Mains

God's Words OF Life on

Joy

*[God] will yet fill your mouth with laughter
and your lips with shouts of joy.*

Job 8:21

*[The Lord's] anger lasts only a moment,
but his favor lasts a lifetime;
weeping may remain for a night,
but rejoicing comes in the morning.*

Psalm 30:5

*Rejoice in the LORD and be glad, you righteous;
sing, all you who are upright in heart!*

Psalm 32:11

Let the righteous rejoice in the LORD
   and take refuge in him;
   let all the upright in heart praise him!
                              Psalm 64:10

May the righteous be glad
   and rejoice before God;
   may they be happy and joyful.
                              Psalm 68:3

May all who seek you
   rejoice and be glad in you;
may those who love your salvation always say,
   "Let God be exalted!"
                              Psalm 70:4

Let all who take refuge in you be glad;
   let them ever sing for joy.
Spread your protection over them,
   that those who love your name may rejoice
      in you.
                              Psalm 5:11

Shout for joy to the LORD, *all the earth.*
   Worship the LORD *with gladness;*
come before him with joyful songs.
                              Psalm 100:1–2

You have made known to me the path of life;
    you will fill me with joy in your presence,
    with eternal pleasures at your right hand,
        [O LORD].

                                    Psalm 16:11

The precepts of the LORD are right,
    giving joy to the heart.
The commands of the LORD are radiant,
    giving light to the eyes.

                                    Psalm 19:8

Those who sow in tears
    will reap with songs of joy.
He who goes out weeping,
    carrying seed to sow,
will return with songs of joy,
    carrying sheaves with him.

                                    Psalm 126:5–6

A cheerful look brings joy to the heart,
    and good news gives health to the bones.

                                    Proverbs 15:30

"You will go out in joy
    and be led forth in peace;

the mountains and hills
    will burst into song before you,
and all the trees of the field
    will clap their hands," the Lord says.
                                    Isaiah 55:12

Rejoice in the LORD your God,
for he has given you
    the autumn rains in righteousness.
He sends you abundant showers,
    both autumn and spring rains, as before.
                                    Joel 2:23

Though the fig tree does not bud
    and there are no grapes on the vines,
though the olive crop fails
    and the fields produce no food,
though there are no sheep in the pen
    and no cattle in the stalls,
yet I will rejoice in the LORD,
    I will be joyful in God my Savior.
                                    Habakkuk 3:17–18

The fruit of the Spirit is love, joy, peace, patience, kindness, goodness, faithfulness, gentleness and self-control.
                                    Galatians 5:22–23

Jesus said, "Until now you have not asked for anything in my name. Ask and you will receive, and your joy will be complete."

John 16:24

Consider it pure joy, my brothers, whenever you face trials of many kinds, because you know that the testing of your faith develops perseverance.

James 1:2–3

Be joyful in hope, patient in affliction, faithful in prayer.

Romans 12:12

The kingdom of God is not a matter of eating and drinking, but of righteousness, peace and joy in the Holy Spirit.

Romans 14:17

May the God of hope fill you with all joy and peace as you trust in him, so that you may overflow with hope by the power of the Holy Spirit.

Romans 15:13

Light is shed upon the righteous
and joy on the upright in heart.

Psalm 97:11

Though you have not seen [Christ], you love him; and even though you do not see him now, you believe in him and are filled with an inexpressible and glorious joy, for you are receiving the goal of your faith, the salvation of your souls.

1 Peter 1:8–9

Rejoice in the Lord always. I will say it again: Rejoice!
Philippians 4:4

The LORD has done great things for us,
and we are filled with joy.

Psalm 126:3

Do not grieve, for the joy of the LORD is your strength.
Nehemiah 8:10

Jesus said,
"Blessed are you when men hate you,
when they exclude you and insult you
and reject your name as evil,
because of the Son of Man.
"Rejoice in that day and leap for joy, because great is your reward in heaven."

Luke 6:22–23

Devotional Thought on Joy

I used to be a little baffled by Nehemiah 8:10: "For the joy of the LORD is your strength."

To me, that verse never made much sense, because joy didn't seem to be all that strong a quality. I thought it would have made more sense if it had said, "The *strength* of the Lord is your *joy*."

But the longer I live, the more I realize that the ability to find joy in life really is a tremendous strength. The people who can laugh are the strong ones. The people who can throw their heads back and delight in the joy of the moment are going to live a lot longer than those of us who are stressed and pushed and taking ourselves terribly seriously.

Children really are good at open-hearted, spontaneous joy. They know it intuitively. That's why they use it lavishly in the present moment. They don't put it in a savings account for a rainy day. They don't put it on hold or put a lid on it. They spend it with abandon. They practice it at every small occasion. That's why they are such pros at getting it right!

Claire Cloninger

God's Words OF Life on

Kindness

Good will come to him who is
generous and lends freely.

Psalm 112:5

Blessed is he who is kind to the needy.

Proverbs 14:21

This is what the LORD Almighty says: "Administer true
justice; show mercy and compassion to one another."

Zechariah 7:9

Jesus said, "Give to the one who asks you, and do not
turn away from the one who wants to borrow from you."

Matthew 5:42

Jesus said, "The King will say to those on his right, 'Come, you who are blessed by my Father; take your inheritance, the kingdom prepared for you since the creation of the world. For I was hungry and you gave me something to eat, I was thirsty and you gave me something to drink, I was a stranger and you invited me in, I needed clothes and you clothed me, I was sick and you looked after me, I was in prison and you came to visit me.'"

Matthew 25:34–36

Live in harmony with one another.

Romans 12:16

As we have opportunity, let us do good to all people, especially to those who belong to the family of believers.

Galatians 6:10

Be kind and compassionate to one another, forgiving each other, just as in Christ God forgave you.

Ephesians 4:32

As God's chosen people, holy and dearly loved, clothe yourselves with compassion, kindness, humility, gentleness and patience.

Colossians 3:12

Live in harmony with one another; be sympathetic, love as brothers, be compassionate and humble. Do not repay evil with evil or insult with insult, but with blessing, because to this you were called so that you may inherit a blessing.

1 Peter 3:8–9

Make every effort to add to your faith goodness; and to goodness, knowledge; and to knowledge, self-control; and to self-control, perseverance; and to perseverance, godliness; and to godliness, brotherly kindness; and to brotherly kindness, love. For if you possess these qualities in increasing measure, they will keep you from being ineffective and unproductive in your knowledge of our Lord Jesus Christ.

2 Peter 1:5–8

Carry each other's burdens, and in this way you will fulfill the law of Christ.

Galatians 6:2

"Let him who boasts boast about this:
that he understands and knows me,
that I am the LORD, who exercises kindness,
justice and righteousness on earth,
for in these I delight," declares the LORD.
Jeremiah 9:24

A kindhearted woman gains respect.

Proverbs 11:16

An anxious heart weighs a man down,
but a kind word cheers him up.

Proverbs 12:25

Jesus said, "In everything, do to others what you would have them do to you, for this sums up the Law and the Prophets."

Matthew 7:12

When the kindness and love of God our Savior appeared, he saved us, not because of righteous things we had done, but because of his mercy.

Titus 3:4–5

Jesus said, "If anyone gives even a cup of cold water to one of these little ones because he is my disciple, I tell you the truth, he will certainly not lose his reward."

Matthew 10:42

Devotional Thought on Kindness

A warm letter from a friend. A compliment from my boss. An unexpected refund.

A comforting scripture. These arrive as God's good gifts to me. But they usually get overlooked while I'm focusing on what feels like—at least to me—insurmountable trouble.

Always, it's trouble that God hasn't solved yet. Often, I complain about his delayed response. But really, my myopic vision isn't fair to him. If I lift my eyes off the problem, I can spot God's gifts all around me.

They may not be the answer I'm searching for at the moment, but they're good and continuous gifts that say, "I still love you, my child." They remind me that God doesn't stop caring for me, even though I live with unfulfilled expectations.

Now during the hard times, I remind myself to hunt for God's small surprises of kindness while I'm waiting for his big solution. It takes my mind off the problem. It helps me to trust him. It encourages me to know that God still cares.

Judith Couchman

Love

The fruit of the Spirit is love, joy, peace, patience, kindness, goodness, faithfulness, gentleness and self-control. Against such things there is no law.

Galatians 5:22–23

God did not give us a spirit of timidity, but a spirit of power, of love and of self-discipline.

2 Timothy 1:7

Whoever does not love does not know God, because God is love.

1 John 4:8

If I speak in the tongues of men and of angels, but have not love, I am only a resounding gong or a clanging cymbal. If I have the gift of prophecy and can fathom all mysteries and all knowledge, and if I have a faith that can move mountains, but have not love, I am nothing. If I give all I possess to the poor and surrender my body to the flames, but have not love, I gain nothing. Love is patient, love is kind. It does not envy, it does not boast, it is not proud. It is not rude, it is not self-seeking, it is not easily angered, it keeps no record of wrongs. Love does not delight in evil but rejoices with the truth. It always protects, always trusts, always hopes, always perseveres. Love never fails.

1 Corinthians 13:1–8

God sends his love and his faithfulness.

Psalm 57:3

Jesus said, "God so loved the world that he gave his one and only Son, that whoever believes in him shall not perish but have eternal life."

John 3:16

Above all, love each other deeply, because love covers over a multitude of sins.

1 Peter 4:8

No one has ever seen God; but if we love one another, God lives in us and his love is made complete in us.

1 John 4:12

"Though the mountains be shaken
and the hills be removed,
yet my unfailing love for you will not be shaken
nor my covenant of peace be removed,"
says the LORD, who has compassion on you.
Isaiah 54:10

Jesus said, "The Father himself loves you because you have loved me and have believed that I came from God."
John 16:27

The LORD is good,
a refuge in times of trouble.
He cares for those who trust in him.
Nahum 1:7

Neither height nor depth, nor anything else in all creation, will be able to separate us from the love of God that is in Christ Jesus our Lord.
Romans 8:39

I pray that out of his glorious riches [God] may strengthen you with power through his Spirit in your inner being, so that Christ may dwell in your hearts through faith. And I pray that you, being rooted and established in love, may have power, together with all the saints, to grasp how wide and long and high and deep is the love of Christ, and to know this love that surpasses knowledge—that you may be filled to the measure of all the fullness of God.

Ephesians 3:16–19

Jesus said, "Love your enemies, do good to them, and lend to them without expecting to get anything back. Then your reward will be great, and you will be sons of the Most High."

Luke 6:35

Love the LORD your God with all your heart and with all your soul and with all your strength.

Deuteronomy 6:5

If anyone acknowledges that Jesus is the Son of God, God lives in him and he in God. And so we know and rely on the love God has for us. God is love. Whoever lives in love lives in God, and God in him.

1 John 4:15–16

Devotional Thought on Love

When I approach the Lord in prayer, I relate to him in different ways. Occasionally I talk with him as my elder brother, which he is. If I'm under spiritual attack, I'll go to him in prayer as the captain of my soul. He is my friend when I want to pour out my heart. I even have single friends who look up to the Lord as their husband, as it says in Isaiah 54:5.

Lately, I've enjoyed relating to my Savior as the lover of my soul. And when I want to tell the Lord how much I adore him, I use the language of love in the Song of Songs. This beautiful book of the Bible is more than just a love poem; it's a picture of the love relationship between the bridegroom and his bride.

From your heart, tell Jesus that he is the fairest of ten thousand. Praise him for being altogether lovely. Let him know that his love is better than wine. He is the rose of Sharon, the lily of the valley.

Joni Eareckson Tada

God's Words OF *Life on*

Loving Others

Jesus said, "My command is this: Love each other as I have loved you. Greater love has no one than this that he lay down his life for his friends."

John 15:12–13

"Do not seek revenge or bear a grudge against one of your people, but love your neighbor as yourself. I am the LORD."

Leviticus 19:18

"The alien living with you must be treated as one of your native-born. Love him as yourself. . . . I am the LORD your God."

Leviticus 19:34

Be devoted to one another in brotherly love. Honor one another above yourselves.

Romans 12:10

Love is patient, love is kind. It does not envy, it does not boast, it is not proud. It is not rude, it is not self-seeking, it is not easily angered, it keeps no record of wrongs. Love does not delight in evil but rejoices with the truth.

1 Corinthians 13:4–6

You . . . were called to be free. But do not use your freedom to indulge the sinful nature; rather, serve one another in love. The entire law is summed up in a single command: "Love your neighbor as yourself."

Galatians 5:13–14

> *How good and pleasant it is*
> *when brothers live together in unity!*
> *Psalm 133:1*

As we have opportunity, let us do good to all people, especially to those who belong to the family of believers.

Galatians 6:10

Live a life of love, just as Christ loved us and gave himself up for us as a fragrant offering and sacrifice to God.

Ephesians 5:2

May the Lord make your love increase and overflow
for each other and for everyone else, just as ours does
for you.

1 Thessalonians 3:12

You yourselves have been taught by God to love
each other.

1 Thessalonians 4:9

If you really keep the royal law found in Scripture,
"Love your neighbor as yourself," you are doing right.

James 2:8

Jesus said, "A new command I give you: Love one
another. As I have loved you, so you must love one
another. By this all men will know that you are my
disciples, if you love one another."

John 13:34–35

Now that you have purified yourselves by obeying the
truth so that you have sincere love for your brothers,
love one another deeply, from the heart.

1 Peter 1:22

All of you, live in harmony with one another; be sympathetic, love as brothers, be compassionate and humble.
Do not repay evil with evil or insult with insult, but

with blessing, because to this you were called so that you may inherit a blessing.

1 Peter 3:8–9

Dear friends, let us love one another, for love comes from God. Everyone who loves has been born of God and knows God.

1 John 4:7

[Christ] has given us this command: Whoever loves God must also love his brother.

1 John 4:21

In Christ Jesus neither circumcision nor uncircumcision has any value. The only thing that counts is faith expressing itself through love.

Galatians 5:6

Devotional Thought on Loving Others

As a teacher teaches best by sparking curiosity, so a friend encourages best by kindling self-worth.

Recently a dear friend was talking with me about her struggles to realize her own worth. "The other day," she said, "I thought of you and another friend who have affirmed me for so many years, believing in me even when I didn't honor my own opinions and feelings, and making me feel special when I didn't place much value on myself. I know where that kind of love comes from. And I know that in time, I'll get better at it too."

What a privilege God has given us to love one another! When the apostle Paul instructed us to observe whatever is true, noble, right, pure, lovely, admirable, excellent, and praiseworthy (Philippians 4:8), he handed us a delightful set of tools to carve self-worth into the lives of others.

As we see and affirm these positive qualities in our friends, our friends begin to see the source of all that is true and excellent and praiseworthy. And soon they begin praising their lovely Creator by becoming all he meant for them to be.

Susan Lenzkes

God's Words
OF Life on

Mercy

He has showed you, O man, what is good.
What does the LORD require of you?
To act justly and to love mercy
and to walk humbly with your God.

Micah 6:8

Jesus said, "Blessed are the merciful,
for they will be shown mercy."

Matthew 5:7

The LORD your God is a merciful God; he will not
abandon or destroy you.

Deuteronomy 4:31

Jesus said, "Be merciful, just as your Father is merciful."

Luke 6:36

We have different gifts, according to the grace given us. . . . If it is encouraging, let him encourage; if it is contributing to the needs of others, let him give generously; if it is leadership, let him govern diligently; if it is showing mercy, let him do it cheerfully.

Romans 12:6, 8

Mercy triumphs over judgment!

James 2:13

The LORD said, "I will cause all my goodness to pass in front of you, and I will proclaim my name, the LORD, in your presence. I will have mercy on whom I will have mercy, and I will have compassion on whom I will have compassion."

Exodus 33:19

Keep yourselves in God's love as you wait for the mercy of our Lord Jesus Christ to bring you to eternal life. Be merciful to those who doubt.

Jude vv. 21–22

The LORD has heard my cry for mercy;
the LORD accepts my prayer.

Psalm 6:9

And [the Lord] passed in front of Moses, proclaiming, "The LORD, the LORD, the compassionate and gracious God, slow to anger, abounding in love and faithfulness, maintaining love to thousands, and forgiving wickedness, rebellion and sin."

Exodus 34:6–7

Do not withhold your mercy from me, O
     LORD;
        may your love and your truth always
        protect me.

Psalm 40:11

Have mercy on me, O God,
        according to your unfailing love;
according to your great compassion
        blot out my transgressions.

Psalm 51:1

Have mercy on me, O God,
        have mercy on me,
        for in you my soul takes refuge.
I will take refuge in the shadow of your wings
        until the disaster has passed.

Psalm 57:1

Answer me, O LORD, out of the
    goodness of your love;
in your great mercy turn to me.

Psalm 69:16

O LORD, hear my prayer,
    listen to my cry for mercy;
in your faithfulness and righteousness
    come to my relief.

Psalm 143:1

In [God's] love and mercy he
    redeemed [his people];
he lifted them up and carried them
    all the days of old.

Isaiah 63:9

The Mighty One has done great things for
        me—
holy is his name.
His mercy extends to those who fear him,
    from generation to generation.

Luke 1:49–50

This is what the LORD Almighty says: "Administer true
justice; show mercy and compassion to one another."

Zechariah 7:9

Because of his great love for us, God, who is rich in mercy, made us alive with Christ even when we were dead in transgressions—it is by grace you have been saved.

Ephesians 2:4–5

The wisdom that comes from heaven is first of all pure; then peace-loving, considerate, submissive, full of mercy and good fruit, impartial and sincere.

James 3:17

He who conceals his sins does not prosper,
but whoever confesses and
renounces them finds mercy.

Proverbs 28:13

Let us then approach the throne of grace with confidence, so that we may receive mercy and find grace to help us in our time of need.

Hebrews 4:16

Who is a God like you,
who pardons sin and
forgives the transgression
of the remnant of his inheritance?
You do not stay angry forever
but delight to show mercy.

Micah 7:18

Let the wicked forsake his way
 and the evil man his thoughts.
Let him turn to the LORD, and
  he will have mercy on him,
 and to our God, for he will freely pardon.
"For my thoughts are not your thoughts,
 neither are your ways my ways,"
  declares the LORD.
"As the heavens are higher than the earth,
 so are my ways higher than your ways
 and my thoughts than your thoughts.
As the rain and the snow
 come down from heaven,
and do not return to it
 without watering the earth
and making it bud and flourish,
 so that it yields seed for the
  sower and bread for the eater,
so is my word that goes out from my mouth:
 It will not return to me empty,
but will accomplish what I desire
 and achieve the purpose for which I sent it."
      Isaiah 55:7–11

"Come now, let us reason together,"
 says the LORD.

"*Though your sins are like scarlet,*
they shall be as white as snow;
though they are red as crimson,
they shall be like wool."

Isaiah 1:18

Devotional Thought on Mercy

Some fishermen in the highlands of Scotland came into a little Scottish inn late one afternoon for a cup of tea.

As one was describing "the one that got away" to his friends, he flung out his hands in the typical fisherman's gesture. He did so just as the waitress was setting down his cup of tea. The resulting collision left a huge tea stain spreading on the whitewashed wall.

The fisherman apologized profusely. Another gentleman seated nearby said, "Never mind."

Rising, he took a crayon from his pocket and began to sketch around the ugly brown stain. Slowly there emerged the head of a magnificent royal stag with antlers spread.

The man was Sir Edwin Henry Landseer, England's foremost painter of animals.

Now, if an artist can do that with an ugly brown stain, what can God do with my sins and mistakes if I but give them to him?

Ruth Bell Graham

God's Words OF Life on

Peace

You will keep in perfect peace
*   him whose mind is steadfast,*
*   because he trusts in you[, Lord].*

Isaiah 26:3

[Christ] himself is our peace, who has made the two one and has destroyed the barrier, the dividing wall of hostility.

Ephesians 2:14

Lord, you establish peace for us;
*   all that we have accomplished you have*
*   done for us.*

Isaiah 26:12

Let the peace of Christ rule in your hearts, since as members of one body you were called to peace. And be thankful.

Colossians 3:15

I will lie down and sleep in peace,
    for you alone, LORD,
    make me dwell in safety.

Psalm 4:8

The LORD gives strength to his people;
    the LORD blesses his people with peace.

Psalm 29:11

Jesus said, "Peace I leave with you; my peace I give you. I do not give to you as the world gives. Do not let your hearts be troubled and do not be afraid."

John 14:27

Do not be anxious about anything, but in every situation, by prayer and petition, with thanksgiving, present your requests to God. And the peace of God, which transcends all understanding, will guard your hearts and your minds in Christ Jesus.

Philippians 4:6–7

Turn from evil and do good;
seek peace and pursue it.

Psalm 34:14

The meek will inherit the land
and enjoy great peace.

Psalm 37:11

Great peace have they who love your law, [LORD,]
and nothing can make them stumble.

Psalm 119:165

The fruit of the Spirit is love, joy, peace, patience, kindness, goodness, faithfulness, gentleness and self-control.

Galatians 5:22–23

There will be trouble and distress for every human being who does evil: . . . but glory, honor and peace for everyone who does good.

Romans 2:9–10

Aim for perfection . . . be of one mind, live in peace. And the God of love and peace will be with you.

2 Corinthians 13:11

Make every effort to keep the unity of the Spirit through the bond of peace.

Ephesians 4:3

When a man's ways are pleasing to the LORD,
he makes even his enemies live at peace
with him.

Proverbs 16:7

If it is possible, as far as it depends on you, live at peace with everyone.

Romans 12:18

The wisdom that comes from heaven is first of all pure; then peace-loving, considerate, submissive, full of mercy and good fruit, impartial and sincere. Peacemakers who sow in peace raise a harvest of righteousness.

James 3:17–18

A heart at peace gives life to the body.

Proverbs 14:30

Let us therefore make every effort to do what leads to peace and to mutual edification.

Romans 14:19

Devotional Thought on Peace

She was just a dishwasher in a restaurant. Part of her duty was the shuttling of dirty dishes to the kitchen and the return of clean ones to the shelves under the counter.

As she was busily arranging these, a man seated at the counter asked her, "Don't you wish your job was piecework?"

She looked up with a questioning look. The term was unfamiliar to her. Then a jagged-toothed smile broke over her expressive face as she replied, "Brother, I'm makin' peace every chance I get! I'm doin' peace work!"

How wonderful! I wish people were more concerned with "peace work" than with "piecework." If God is our peace, then we should be peacemakers. An overemphasis on piecework to gain wages rather than peace work for an eternal inheritance can never bring satisfaction.

Where is your life's emphasis?

Kathryn Hillen

God's Words OF Life on

Perspective

"My thoughts are not your thoughts,
neither are your ways my ways,"
declares the LORD.
"As the heavens are higher than the earth,
so are my ways higher than your ways
and my thoughts than your thoughts."
Isaiah 55:8–9

All the ways of the Lord are loving and faithful.
Psalm 25:10

Praise and exalt and glorify the King of heaven, because everything he does is right and all his ways are just. And those who walk in pride he is able to humble.
Daniel 4:37

Your love, O LORD, *reaches to the heavens,*
    your faithfulness to the skies.

Psalm 36:5

I will remember the deeds of the LORD;
        yes, I will remember your
            miracles of long ago. . . .
Your path led through the sea,
    your way through the mighty waters,
    though your footprints were not seen.

Psalm 77:11, 19

I will declare that your love stands firm forever,
    that you established your faithfulness
in heaven itself[, LORD].

Psalm 89:2

As high as the heavens are above the earth,
    so great is [God's] love for those who fear him.

Psalm 103:11

Oh, the depth of the riches of the wisdom
        and knowledge of God!
    How unsearchable his judgments,
    and his paths beyond tracing out!
"Who has known the mind of the Lord?
    Or who has been his counselor?"

"Who has ever given to God,
        that God should repay him?"
For from him and through him and to him
            are all things.
To him be the glory forever! Amen.

Romans 11:33–36

"The LORD does not look at the things man looks at.
Man looks at the outward appearance, but the LORD
looks at the heart," says the Lord.

1 Samuel 16:7

Do you not know?
    Have you not heard?
The LORD is the everlasting God,
    the Creator of the ends of the earth.
He will not grow tired or weary,
    and his understanding no one can fathom.
He gives strength to the weary
    and increases the power of the weak.

Isaiah 40:28–29

How great are your works, O LORD,
    how profound your thoughts!

Psalm 92:5

The LORD longs to be gracious to you;
he rises to show you compassion.
For the LORD is a God of justice.
Blessed are all who wait for him!

Isaiah 30:18

"I know the plans I have for you," declares the LORD, "plans to prosper you and not to harm you, plans to give you hope and a future."

Jeremiah 29:11

Jesus said, "If you . . . know how to give good gifts to your children, how much more will your Father in heaven give good gifts to those who ask him!"

Matthew 7:11

Jesus said, "Surely I am with you always, to the very end of the age."

Matthew 28:20

The plans of the LORD stand firm forever,
the purposes of his heart through all generations.

Psalm 33:11

Devotional Thought on Perspective

The Old Testament kingdom of Judah needed a kick in the pants, a shot in the arm, a knock on the head. They had rebelled against God, for which God plainly and directly judged them through the prophet Isaiah and through foreign nations. They deserved to be scolded or punished, but God was as wise then as he is now. He simply opened their eyes.

"Your vision is too small because of your pain," he said. "You've focused on your lack. Hang it all! Expand your tent pegs out a few notches and live as if you have it all. Because you do! You have my undying love. My forgiveness. My power. You have me!"

There are days when I need such a vision. I tire easily at times. And when I tire I want to go into my "tents" of pity and frustration and anger. My small tents are comfortable. Though they are dark and cramped, I feel a sense of comfort. But not for long.

God desires my company under a larger tent that I might expand his kingdom with him.

And as I do so, I find the fresh breeze of new strength to deal with my pity, frustration and anger. I am renewed.

Joni Eareckson Tada

God's Words OF Life on

Prayer

"Before they call I will answer;
while they are still speaking I will hear,"
says the LORD.

Isaiah 65:24

Jesus answered, "Whatever you ask for in prayer, believe that you have received it, and it will be yours."

Mark 11:24

Jesus said, "Ask and it will be given to you; seek and you will find; knock and the door will be opened to you. For everyone who asks receives; he who seeks finds; and to him who knocks, the door will be opened."

Matthew 7:7–8

Jesus said, "If you believe, you will receive whatever you ask for in prayer."

Matthew 21:22

Jesus said, "I tell you that if two of you on earth agree about anything you ask for, it will be done for you by my Father in heaven. For where two or three come together in my name, there am I with them."

Matthew 18:19–20

Jesus said, "When you pray, go into your room, close the door and pray to your Father, who is unseen. Then Your Father, who sees what is done in secret, will reward you."

Matthew 6:6

"Call to me and I will answer you and tell you great and unsearchable things you do not know," says the Lord.

Jeremiah 33:3

"He will call upon me, and I will answer him;
I will be with him in trouble,
I will deliver him and honor him,"
says the Lord.

Psalm 91:15

The LORD . . . hears the prayer of the righteous.
Proverbs 15:29

Delight yourself in the LORD
*   and he will give you the desires of your*
*   heart.*

Psalm 37:4

Let us then approach the throne of grace with confidence, so that we may receive mercy and find grace to help us in our time of need.

Hebrews 4:16

Jesus said, "I tell you the truth, my Father will give you whatever you ask in my name. Until now you have not asked for anything in my name. Ask and you will receive, and your joy will be complete."

John 16:23–24

The LORD is near to all who call on him,
*   to all who call on him in truth.*

Psalm 145:18

Jesus said, "If you remain in me and my words remain in you, ask whatever you wish, and it will be given you."

John 15:7

Jesus said, "I will do whatever you ask in my name, so that the Son may bring glory to the Father. You may ask me for anything in my name, and I will do it."

John 14:13–14

"If my people, who are called by my name, will humble themselves and pray and seek my face and turn from their wicked ways, then will I hear from heaven and will forgive their sin and will heal their land," says the Lord.

2 Chronicles 7:14

I wait for you, O LORD;
*   you will answer, O Lord my God.*

Psalm 38:15

If we confess our sins, [God] is faithful and just and will forgive us our sins and purify us from all unrighteousness.

1 John 1:9

Very early in the morning, while it was still dark, Jesus got up, left the house and went off to a solitary place, where he prayed.

Mark 1:35

Do not be anxious about anything, but in everything, by prayer and petition, with thanksgiving, present your requests to God.

And the peace of God, which transcends all understanding, will guard your hearts and your minds in Christ Jesus.

Philippians 4:6–7

Is any one of you in trouble? He should pray. Is anyone happy? Let him sing songs of praise. Is any one of you sick? He should call the elders of the church to pray over him and anoint him with oil in the name of the Lord. And the prayer offered in faith will make the sick person well; the Lord will raise him up. If he has sinned, he will be forgiven. Therefore confess your sins to each other and pray for each other so that you may be healed. The prayer of a righteous man is powerful and effective.

James 5:13–16

This is the confidence we have in approaching God: that if we ask anything according to his will, he hears us. And if we know that he hears us—whatever we ask—we know that we have what we asked of him.

1 John 5:14–15

"I know the plans I have for you," declares the LORD, "plans to prosper you and not to harm you, plans to give you hope and a future. Then you will call upon me and come and pray to me, and I will listen to you. You will seek me and find me when you seek me with all your heart."

Jeremiah 29:11–13

The eyes of the Lord are on the righteous
and his ears are attentive to their prayer.
1 Peter 3:12

Jesus said, "This, then, is how you should pray:
'Our Father in heaven,
hallowed be your name,
your kingdom come,
your will be done
on earth as it is in heaven.
Give us today our daily bread.
Forgive us our debts,
as we also have forgiven our debtors.
And lead us not into temptation,
but deliver us from the evil one.'"

Matthew 6:9–13

Devotional Thought on Prayer

"What do you want?" Jesus asks you.

It is such a simple question, and yet you know that how you answer that question is going to shape the rest of your days.

Standing there, poised between your old life and the future, you feel alive as never before. Time seems to stand still. All the colors around you are vivid; the sounds are clear and almost musical.

What do you say when Jesus asks what you want? Do you even know what you want? As you stand there, enclosed in a holy space even in the midst of a crowd, you examine your heart.

Are you coming to Jesus out of curiosity? Do you have some need you think he might meet or an intellectual question he might answer? Is there something in you that needs to be healed? Is there some brokenness, a piercing or unrelenting pain, a failure from your past that you would like him to carry? Do you need forgiveness? Is there something you have tried to fix that escapes your skill?

Exactly what is it that you want from Jesus of Nazareth? Tell him, in your prayer of the heart, exactly what you need.

Jeanie Miley

God's Words OF Life on

Relationships

Be completely humble and gentle; be patient, bearing
with one another in love. Make every effort to keep the
unity of the Spirit through the bond of peace.

Ephesians 4:2–3

Bear with each other and forgive whatever grievances
you may have against one another. Forgive as the Lord
forgave you.

Colossians 3:13

Jesus replied: "'Love the Lord your God with all your
heart and with all your soul and with all your mind.'
This is the first and greatest commandment. And the
second is like it: 'Love your neighbor as yourself.'"

Matthew 22:37–39

By the grace given me I say to every one of you: Do not think of yourself more highly than you ought, but rather think of yourself with sober judgment, in accordance with the measure of faith God has given you. Just as each of us has one body with many members, and these members do not all have the same function, so in Christ we who are many form one body, and each member belongs to all the others.

Romans 12:3–5

Two are better than one,
    because they have a good return for their
        work:
If one falls down,
    his friend can help him up.
But pity the man who falls
    and has no one to help him up! . . .
Though one may be overpowered,
    two can defend themselves.
A cord of three strands is not quickly broken.
        Ecclesiastes 4:9–12

In everything set them an example by doing what is good. In your teaching show integrity, seriousness and soundness of speech that cannot be condemned, so that those who oppose you may be ashamed because they have nothing bad to say about us.

Titus 2:7–8

Therefore, as we have opportunity, let us do good to all people, especially to those who belong to the family of believers.

Galatians 6:10

As iron sharpens iron,
*   so one man sharpens another.*

Proverbs 27:17

As believers in our glorious Lord Jesus Christ, don't show favoritism.

James 2:1

Jesus said, "By this all men will know that you are my disciples, if you love one another."

John 13:35

A man of many companions may come to ruin,
*   but there is a friend who sticks closer*
*   than a brother.*

Proverbs 18:24

He who walks with the wise grows wise,
but a companion of fools suffers harm.

Proverbs 13:20

Jesus said, "Whoever wants to become great among you must be your servant, and whoever wants to be first must be your slave—just as the Son of Man did not come to be served, but to serve, and to give his life as a ransom for many."

Matthew 20:26–28

Carry each other's burdens, and in this way you will fulfill the law of Christ.

Galatians 6:2

Give everyone what you owe him: If you owe taxes, pay taxes; if revenue, then revenue; if respect, then respect; if honor, then honor. Let no debt remain outstanding, except the continuing debt to love one another.

Romans 13:7–8

Peacemakers who sow in peace raise a harvest of righteousness.

James 3:18

Love one another deeply, from the heart.

1 Peter 1:22

All of you, clothe yourselves with humility toward one another, because,

> "*God opposes the proud*
> *but gives grace to the humble.*"

Humble yourselves, therefore, under God's mighty hand, that he may lift you up in due time.

1 Peter 5:5–6

We ask you, brothers, to respect those who work hard among you, who are over you in the Lord and who admonish you. Hold them in the highest regard in love because of their work. Live in peace with each other.

1 Thessalonians 5:12–13

I appeal to you, brothers, in the name of our Lord Jesus Christ, that all of you agree with one another so that there may be no divisions among you and that you may be perfectly united in mind and thought.

1 Corinthians 1:10

A man's wisdom gives him patience;
> *it is to his glory to overlook an offense.*

Proverbs 19:11

Devotional Thought on Relationships

Unlike jigsaw puzzles, people don't always fit together perfectly. Everyone's personality has unique ins and outs.

Some are busy, get-it-done types, for whom people are a means to an end. Others are more laid-back; they talk about getting something done, but never quite get to it. To them, people and relationships *are* the end.

When these two types get together, they can despair over the other's failure, blind to their own. Or they can see those conflicts as opportunities for their own growth.

In my family, cartoons help us celebrate our differences and help us be patient with one another. Any comic strip that hits home is clipped and posted on the refrigerator for laughs. Then I paste it in a notebook, kept with the family photo albums, for repeat laughs and long-term reminders of how human we all really are.

Jeanne Zornes

God's Words
OF Life on

Rest

Jesus said, "Come to me, all you who are weary and burdened, and I will give you rest. Take my yoke upon you and learn from me, for I am gentle and humble in heart, and you will find rest for your souls. For my yoke is easy and my burden is light."

Matthew 11:28–30

Let us not become weary in doing good, for at the proper time we will reap a harvest if we do not give up.

Galatians 6:9

The LORD replied, "My Presence will go with you, and I will give you rest."

Exodus 33:14

You are awesome, O God, in your sanctuary;
the God of Israel gives power
and strength to his people.
Praise be to God!

Psalm 68:35

[God] gives strength to the weary
and increases the power of the weak.
Even youths grow tired and weary,
and young men stumble and fall;
but those who hope in the LORD
will renew their strength.
They will soar on wings like eagles;
they will run and not grow weary,
they will walk and not be faint.

Isaiah 40:29–31

"Do not fear, for I am with you;
do not be dismayed, for I am your God.
I will strengthen you and help you;
I will uphold you with my righteous right
hand."

Isaiah 41:10

"I will refresh the weary and satisfy the faint," says
the Lord.

Jeremiah 31:25

Unless the LORD builds the house,
*   its builders labor in vain.*
Unless the LORD watches over the city,
*   the watchmen stand guard in vain.*
In vain you rise early
*   and stay up late,*
toiling for food to eat—
*   for he grants sleep to those he loves.*

*   Psalm 127:1–2*

"Remember the Sabbath day by keeping it holy. Six days you shall labor and do all your work, but the seventh day is a Sabbath to the LORD your God. On it you shall not do any work, neither you, nor your son or daughter, nor your manservant or maidservant, nor your animals, nor the alien within your gates. For in six days the LORD made the heavens and the earth, the sea, and all that is in them, but he rested on the seventh day. Therefore the LORD blessed the Sabbath day and made it holy," says the Lord.

*   Exodus 20:8–11*

[The LORD] makes me lie down in green
*   pastures,*
he leads me beside quiet waters,
*   he restores my soul.*

He guides me in paths of righteousness
for his name's sake.

Psalm 23:2–3

Let the beloved of the LORD rest secure in him,
for he shields him all day long,
and the one the LORD loves
rests between his shoulders.

Deuteronomy 33:12

There remains, then, a Sabbath-rest for the people of God; for anyone who enters God's rest also rests from his own work, just as God did from his. Let us, therefore, make every effort to enter that rest.

Hebrews 4:9–11

He who dwells in the shelter of the Most High
will rest in the shadow of the Almighty.

Psalm 91:1

Because so many people were coming and going that they did not even have a chance to eat, [Jesus] said to them, "Come with me by yourselves to a quiet place and get some rest."

Mark 6:31

Devotional Thought on Rest

Are you exhausted today? Are you taking pills for energy to get through the day? Or are you on a nervous high and need something to slow you down? Perhaps what your body is really crying for is rest. Is there rest for anyone in this tension-filled world?

As the disciples returned from a missionary journey, they were elated with their success. They gave glowing reports of how God had worked. Jesus was glad to hear their accounts, but he knew that they needed physical rest after their arduous journey. He invited them to come rest with him in a quiet place.

We, too, need to refresh ourselves to maintain physical and spiritual strength. Our schedules are demanding. They drain our physical, mental, emotional, and spiritual life.

God's Holy Spirit gives us strength for his schedule for us. I believe God plans for us to include times of rest and relaxation in our schedule. If the disciples needed rest, so do we.

Our rest times may consist of a vacation where we can rest and relax, a change of environment, or simply a respite right where we are. Time spent with the Lord brings renewal and refreshment.

Millie Stamm

Self-Worth

God said, "Let us make man in our image, in our likeness, and let them rule over the fish of the sea and the birds of the air, over the livestock, over all the earth, and over all the creatures that move along the ground."

So God created man in his own image, in the image of God he created him; male and female he created them.

Genesis 1:26–27

What is man that you are mindful of him,
the son of man that you care for him?
You made him a little lower than the heavenly
beings

and crowned him with glory and honor.
You made him ruler over the works of your
hands;
you put everything under his feet.

Psalm 8:4–6

How precious to me are your thoughts, O God!
How vast is the sum of them!
Were I to count them,
they would outnumber the grains of sand.
When I awake,
I am still with you.

Psalm 139:17–18

"Before I formed you in the womb I knew you,
before you were born I set you apart,"
says the Lord.

Jeremiah 1:5

Do you not know that your body is a temple of the
Holy Spirit, who is in you, whom you have received
from God? You are not your own; you were bought at
a price. Therefore honor God with your body.

1 Corinthians 6:19–20

Jesus said, "Are not two sparrows sold for a penny? Yet not one of them will fall to the ground apart from the will of your Father. And even the very hairs of your head are all numbered. So don't be afraid; you are worth more than many sparrows."

Matthew 10:29–31

You created my inmost being;
    you knit me together in my mother's womb.
I praise you because I am fearfully and
        wonderfully made;
    your works are wonderful,
    I know that full well.

Psalm 139:13–14

From one man [God] made every nation of men, that they should inhabit the whole earth; and he determined the times set for them and the exact places where they should live. . . . "For in him we live and move and have our being." As some of your own poets have said, "We are God's offspring."

Acts 17:26, 28

I pray that out of [God's] glorious riches he may strengthen you with power through his Spirit in your inner being, so that Christ may dwell in your hearts through faith. And I pray that you, being rooted and established in love, may have power, together with all the saints, to grasp how wide and long and high and deep is the love of Christ, and to know this love that surpasses knowledge—that you may be filled to the measure of all the fullness of God.

Ephesians 3:16–19

We are God's workmanship, created in Christ Jesus to do good works, which God prepared in advance for us to do.

Ephesians 2:10

Devotional Thought on Self-Worth

An unhealthy and unrealistic sense of self can make our lives miserable and even ruin our health. I have known more than one anorexic teen who has stubbornly tried to starve herself because she saw her thin body as fat.

We try to acquire a feeling of significance in many other areas as well: our work, our achievements, our bank accounts, our social standing, our "connections." Adam and Eve in the garden did not need any of these things to prove their value. But our chaotic culture has us running around in circles trying to find our worth in doing.

The year I worked in the advertising industry, I saw firsthand that fortunes are made and empires built on the shaky self-images of prospective consumers. Every ad I wrote was aimed at convincing buyers that with one simple purchase they would magically possess the self-confidence they had been lacking.

But the truth is, no amount of money can buy back for us that true, balanced, sense of self-worth that was left behind in Eden. It can only be found where Adam and Eve found it—in the eyes of the One who made us.

Claire Cloninger

God's Words OF Life on

Speech

A man finds joy in giving an apt reply—
  and how good is a timely word!
                    Proverbs 15:23

From the fruit of his lips a man is filled
  with good things
as surely as the work of his hands rewards him.
                    Proverbs 12:14

Do not let any unwholesome talk come out of your mouths, but only what is helpful for building others up according to their needs, that it may benefit those who listen.

                    Ephesians 4:29

Jesus said, "Out of the overflow of the heart the mouth speaks."

Matthew 12:34

Let your conversation be always full of grace, seasoned with salt, so that you may know how to answer everyone.

Colossians 4:6

> *Whoever of you loves life*
> *and desires to see many good days,*
> *keep your tongue from evil*
> *and your lips from speaking lies.*
> *Turn from evil and do good;*
> *seek peace and pursue it.*

Psalm 34:12–14

We all stumble in many ways. If anyone is never at fault in what he says, he is a perfect man, able to keep his whole body in check. When we put bits into the mouths of horses to make them obey us, we can turn the whole animal. . . . Likewise the tongue is a small part of the body, but it makes great boasts. Consider what a great forest is set on fire by a small spark.

James 3:2–3, 5

> *An honest answer*
> *is like a kiss on the lips.*

Proverbs 24:26

Do everything without complaining or arguing.
Philippians 2:14

Do your best to present yourself to God as one approved, a workman who does not need to be ashamed and who correctly handles the word of truth.
2 Timothy 2:15

The mouth of the righteous man utters wisdom,
and his tongue speaks what is just.
Psalm 37:30

May my lips overflow with praise,
for you teach me your decrees.
May my tongue sing of your word,
for all your commands are righteous.
Psalm 119:171–172

He who guards his lips guards his life,
but he who speaks rashly will come to ruin.
Proverbs 13:3

The tongue has the power of life and death,
and those who love it will eat its fruit.
Proverbs 18:21

The tongue of the righteous is choice silver.
Proverbs 10:20

Speaking the truth in love, we will in all things grow up into him who is the Head, that is, Christ.

Ephesians 4:15

A word aptly spoken
is like apples of gold in settings of silver.

Proverbs 25:11

Devotional Thought on Speech

Imparting the truth is not easy. There is a right moment to speak—not at the end of an exhausting day. Sometimes it would be better to listen. The speaker must ask herself if this truth will be an encouragement, a positive force for growth.

Ephesians 4:15 tells us to speak "the truth in love." Our attitudes toward our listeners affect how our words will be received. The tone of voice and the look in a person's eyes can convey concern. Yet the truth, even from Scripture, can hurt and can subsequently be rejected if spoken from an unloving heart. The simile of truth as a two-edged sword is intended for use on our enemies, not our friends.

The "apples of gold in settings of silver" (Proverbs 25:11) are thought to be golden balls arranged in silver filigree baskets. These were set on the table as ornaments, much like we use centerpieces today. No doubt they were carefully handcrafted, valuable, and very beautiful.

So should our words be.

Jean Shaw

Talents and Abilities

Remember the LORD your God, for it is he who gives
you the ability to produce wealth.

Deuteronomy 8:18

> *The LORD God is a sun and shield;*
> *the LORD bestows favor and honor;*
> *no good thing does he withhold*
> *from those whose walk is blameless.*
>
> *Psalm 84:11*

To the man who pleases him, God gives wisdom,
knowledge and happiness.

Ecclesiastes 2:26

Don't let anyone look down on you because you are
young, but set an example for the believers in speech,
in life, in love, in faith and in purity. Until I come,

devote yourself to the public reading of Scripture, to preaching and to teaching. Do not neglect your gift.

1 Timothy 4:12–14

Every good and perfect gift is from above, coming down from the Father of the heavenly lights, who does not change like shifting shadows.

James 1:17

God's gifts and his call are irrevocable.

Romans 11:29

We have different gifts, according to the grace given us. If a man's gift is prophesying, let him use it in proportion to his faith. If it is serving, let him serve; if it is teaching, let him teach; if it is encouraging, let him encourage; if it is contributing to the needs of others, let him give generously; if it is leadership, let him govern diligently; if it is showing mercy, let him do it cheerfully.

Romans 12:6–8

In [God] you have been enriched in every way—in all your speaking and in all your knowledge.

1 Corinthians 1:5

Each man has his own gift from God; one has this gift, another has that.

1 Corinthians 7:7

Each one should use whatever gift he has received to serve others, faithfully administering God's grace in its various forms.

1 Peter 4:10

There are different kinds of gifts, but the same Spirit. There are different kinds of service, but the same Lord. There are different kinds of working, but the same God works all of them in all men. Now to each one the manifestation of the Spirit is given for the common good. To one there is given through the Spirit the message of wisdom, to another the message of knowledge by means of the same Spirit, to another faith by the same Spirit, to another gifts of healing by that one Spirit, to another miraculous powers, to another prophecy, to another distinguishing between spirits, to another speaking in different kinds of tongues, and to still another the interpretation of tongues. All these are the work of one and the same Spirit, and he gives them to each one, just as he determines.

1 Corinthians 12:4–11

May [the LORD] give you the desire of your heart
and make all your plans succeed.

Psalm 20:4

Devotional Thought on Talents and Abilities

I have known my daughter-in-law, Judi, since she was a teenager. Watching her grow into a mature and creative adult has been a pleasure. She is a successful singer, wife, mother, and dress designer. Her home is a masterpiece design of her creation.

I remember when Judi felt like she could do very little, and had few talents to offer the Lord. The truth is, God has given talents to each of us. We cannot all sing or design a home that looks like Judi's, but we can develop the talents God gives us for his glory.

Life is an ongoing process, a gradual growth in grace and in the talents God has placed within us. The talents we use change from season to season so there is a lifetime to develop them. God will bring to the surface at the proper time talents that laid dormant for years.

As we press on in our walk with God, we realize that what he has for us is far too much to cram into the first thirty, forty, or fifty years of our lives. Keep on looking for and developing new talents. God will bring them out in you, as you yield yourself to him.

Nancy Corbett Cole

God's Words OF Life on

Thankfulness

The trumpeters and singers joined in unison, as with one voice, to give praise and thanks to the LORD. Accompanied by trumpets, cymbals and other instruments, they raised their voices in praise to the LORD and sang:

"He is good;
    his love endures forever."
Then the temple of the LORD was filled with a cloud.

2 Chronicles 5:13

I will give thanks to the LORD
    because of his righteousness
and will sing praise to the name
    of the LORD Most High.

Psalm 7:17

The LORD is my strength and my shield;
    my heart trusts in him, and I am helped.
My heart leaps for joy
    and I will give thanks to him in song.
                                        Psalm 28:7

O LORD my God, I will give you thanks forever.
                                        Psalm 30:12

But thanks be to God, who always leads us in triumphal procession in Christ and through us spreads everywhere the fragrance of the knowledge of him.
                                        2 Corinthians 2:14

Let the peace of Christ rule in your hearts, since as members of one body you were called to peace. And be thankful. Let the word of Christ dwell in you richly as you teach and admonish one another with all wisdom, and as you sing psalms, hymns and spiritual songs with gratitude in your hearts to God. And whatever you do, whether in word or deed, do it all in the name of the Lord Jesus, giving thanks to God the Father through him.
                                        Colossians 3:15–17

Devote yourselves to prayer, being watchful and thankful.
                                        Colossians 4:2

The LORD gave and the LORD has taken away;
may the name of the LORD be praised.

Job 1:21

I will extol the LORD at all times;
his praise will always be on my lips.

Psalm 34:1

Thanks be to God for his indescribable gift!

2 Corinthians 9:15

Do not be anxious about anything, but in everything, by prayer and petition, with thanksgiving, present your requests to God.

Philippians 4:6

Give thanks in all circumstances, for this is God's will for you in Christ Jesus.

1 Thessalonians 5:18

Thanks be to God! He gives us the victory through our Lord Jesus Christ.

1 Corinthians 15:57

Give thanks to the LORD, call on his name;
make known among the nations
what he has done.

1 Chronicles 16:8

Praise the LORD.
I will extol the LORD with all my heart
in the council of the upright
and in the assembly.
Great are the works of the LORD;
they are pondered by all who delight in them.
                                        Psalm 111:1–2

Sing and make music in your heart to the Lord, always giving thanks to God the Father for everything, in the name of our Lord Jesus Christ.

                                        Ephesians 5:19–20

Just as you received Christ Jesus as Lord, continue to live in him, rooted and built up in him, strengthened in the faith as you were taught, and overflowing with thankfulness.

                                        Colossians 2:6–7

Sing to the LORD with thanksgiving;
make music to our God on the harp.
                                        Psalm 147:7

Enter [God's] gates with thanksgiving
and his courts with praise;
give thanks to him and praise his name.
                                        Psalm 100:4

Since we are receiving a kingdom that cannot be shaken, let us be thankful, and so worship God acceptably with reverence and awe.

Hebrews 12:28

Everything God created is good, and nothing is to be rejected if it is received with thanksgiving.

1 Timothy 4:4

Through Jesus, therefore, let us continually offer to God a sacrifice of praise—the fruit of lips that confess his name.

Hebrews 13:15

We give thanks to you, O God,
we give thanks, for your Name is near;
men tell of your wonderful deeds.

Psalm 75:1

We always thank God for all of you, mentioning you in our prayers. We continually remember before our God and Father your work produced by faith, your labor prompted by love, and your endurance inspired by hope in our Lord Jesus Christ.

1 Thessalonians 1:2–3

*Praise and glory
and wisdom and thanks and honor
and power and strength
be to our God for ever and ever.
Amen!*

Revelation 7:12

Devotional Thought on Thankfulness

The spirit of celebration finds a natural expression in parties and get-togethers, times of laughter and revelry. But the celebrating spirit need not limit itself to party time.

The spirit of celebration is for all of our lives.

This means that celebration shows itself in little moments of grace as well as in rambunctious revelry. It smiles in a geranium on a sunlit windowsill as well as in a cookout at the beach. Most of all, celebration shines in quiet gratitude that God has blessed our homes and our lives with the spirit of loveliness. We celebrate because our lives overflow with things to be thankful for, and because God gives us the eyes to see how incredibly we have been blessed.

There are so many ways to celebrate God's gifts of our lives and our relationships—and of himself! We celebrate when we take the time to nurture ourselves and our families. We celebrate through our willingness to share, to love each other, to grow. And we celebrate by opening our lives to the Lord and letting his Spirit fill our lives with loveliness.

Emilie Barnes

God's Words
OF Life on

Trust

Those who know your name will trust in you,
for you, LORD, have never forsaken
those who seek you.

Psalm 9:10

Blessed is the man who trusts in the LORD,
whose confidence is in him.
He will be like a tree planted by the water
that sends out its roots by the stream.
It does not fear when heat comes;
its leaves are always green.
It has no worries in a year of drought
and never fails to bear fruit.

Jeremiah 17:7–8

[Abraham] did not waver through unbelief regarding the promise of God, but was strengthened in his faith and gave glory to God, being fully persuaded that God had power to do what he had promised.

Romans 4:20–21

Taste and see that the LORD is good;
  blessed is the man who takes refuge in him.

Psalm 34:8

O LORD Almighty,
  blessed is the man who trusts in you.

Psalm 84:12

Blessed is he whose help is the God of Jacob,
  whose hope is in the LORD his God.

Psalm 146:5

Whoever gives heed to instruction prospers,
  and blessed is he who trusts in the LORD.

Proverbs 16:20

You will keep in perfect peace
  him whose mind is steadfast,
  because he trusts in you.
Trust in the LORD forever,
  for the LORD, the LORD, is the Rock eternal.

Isaiah 26:3–4

The LORD longs to be gracious to you;
*   he rises to show you compassion.*
For the LORD is a God of justice.
*   Blessed are all who wait for him!*
                                    Isaiah 30:18

The eternal God is your refuge,
*   and underneath are the everlasting arms.*
                                Deuteronomy 33:27

The LORD's unfailing love
*   surrounds the man who trusts in him.*
                                    Psalm 32:10

Those who trust in the LORD are like Mount
*   Zion,*
*   which cannot be shaken but endures forever.*
                                    Psalm 125:1

Blessed is the man
*   who makes the LORD his trust,*
who does not look to the proud,
*   to those who turn aside to false gods.*
                                    Psalm 40:4

Anyone who trusts in God will never be put to shame.
                                    Romans 10:11

*Trust in the L*ORD *with all your heart*
    and lean not on your own understanding;
in all your ways acknowledge him,
    and he will make your paths straight.

Proverbs 3:5–6

A greedy man stirs up dissension,
    *but he who trusts in the L*ORD *will prosper.*

Proverbs 28:25

Nebuchadnezzar said, "Praise be to the God of Shadrach, Meshach and Abednego, who has sent his angel and rescued his servants! They trusted in him and defied the king's command and were willing to give up their lives rather than serve or worship any god except their own God."

Daniel 3:28

Be strong and take heart,
    *all you who hope in the L*ORD.

Psalm 31:24

Fear of man will prove to be a snare,
    *but whoever trusts in the L*ORD *is kept safe.*

Proverbs 29:25

Trust in him at all times, O people;
    pour out your hearts to him,
    for God is our refuge.

Psalm 62:8

The LORD is good,
    a refuge in times of trouble.
He cares for those who trust in him.

Nahum 1:7

I will lie down and sleep in peace,
    for you alone, O LORD,
    make me dwell in safety.

Psalm 4:8

In you I trust, O my God.
Do not let me be put to shame,
    nor let my enemies triumph over me.
No one whose hope is in you
    will ever be put to shame,
but they will be put to shame
    who are treacherous without excuse.
Show me your ways, O LORD,
    teach me your paths;
guide me in your truth and teach me,
    for you are God my Savior,
and my hope is in you all day long.

Psalm 25:2–5

Trust in the LORD and do good;
  dwell in the land and enjoy safe pasture.
Delight yourself in the LORD
  and he will give you the desires of your
    heart.
Commit your way to the LORD;
  trust in him and he will do this:
He will make your righteousness
    shine like the dawn,
  the justice of your cause like
    the noonday sun.

Psalm 37:3–6

I trust in your unfailing love;
  My heart rejoices in your salvation.
I will sing to the LORD,
  for he has been good to me.

Psalm 13:5–6

Devotional Thought on Trust

No person or company of people, no power in earth or heaven, can touch that soul that is abiding in Christ, without first passing through his encircling presence, and receiving the seal of his permission. If God be for us, it matters not who may be against us; nothing can disturb or harm us, except God shall see that it is best for us, and shall stand aside to let it pass.

An earthly parent's care for his helpless child is a feeble illustration of this. If the child is in its father's arms, nothing can touch it without that father's consent, unless he is too weak to prevent it. If an earthly parent would thus care for his little helpless one, how much more will our heavenly Father, whose love is infinitely greater, and whose strength and wisdom can never be baffled, care for us!

What is needed, then, is to see God in everything, and to receive everything directly from his hands, with no intervention of second causes; and it is to just this that we must be brought before we can know an abiding experience of entire abandonment and perfect trust.

Hannah Whitall Smith

God's Words OF Life on

Values

Jesus said, "In everything, do to others what you would have them do to you, for this sums up the Law and the Prophets."

Matthew 7:12

Jesus replied: "'Love the Lord your God with all your heart and with all your soul and with all your mind.' This is the first and greatest commandment. And the second is like it: 'Love your neighbor as yourself.' All the Law and the Prophets hang on these two commandments."

Matthew 22:37–40

As God's chosen people, holy and dearly loved, clothe yourselves with compassion, kindness, humility, gentleness and patience. Bear with each other and forgive whatever grievances you may have against one another.

Forgive as the Lord forgave you. And over all these virtues put on love, which binds them all together in perfect unity.

Colossians 3:12–14

The fruit of the Spirit is love, joy, peace, patience, kindness, goodness, faithfulness, gentleness and self-control.

Galatians 5:22–23

He has showed you, O man, what is good.
    And what does the LORD require of you?
To act justly and to love mercy
    and to walk humbly with your God.

Micah 6:8

Physical training is of some value, but godliness has value for all things, holding promise for both the present life and the life to come.

1 Timothy 4:8

Who may ascend the hill of the LORD?
    Who may stand in his holy place?
He who has clean hands and a pure heart,
    who does not lift up his soul to an idol
    or swear by what is false.

Psalm 24:3–4

Two things I ask of you, O LORD;
*   do not refuse me before I die:*
Keep falsehood and lies far from me;
*   give me neither poverty nor riches,*
*   but give me only my daily bread.*
* Otherwise, I may have too much and disown*
*   you*
*   and say, "Who is the LORD?"*
Or I may become poor and steal,
*   and so dishonor the name of my God.*
*   Proverbs 30:7–9*

Better a poor man whose walk is blameless
*   than a rich man whose ways are perverse.*
*   Proverbs 28:6*

We also rejoice in our sufferings, because we know that
suffering produces perseverance; perseverance, character; and character, hope.

Romans 5:3–4

Be careful that you do not forget the LORD your God,
failing to observe his commands, his laws and his
decrees that I am giving you this day.

Deuteronomy 8:11

The LORD rewards every man for his righteousness and faithfulness.

1 Samuel 26:23

Make every effort to live in peace with all men and to be holy; without holiness no one will see the Lord. See to it that no one misses the grace of God and that no bitter root grows up to cause trouble and defile many.

Hebrews 12:14–15

> *This is what the LORD says:*
> *"Stand at the crossroads and look;*
> *ask for the ancient paths,*
> *ask where the good way is, and walk in it,*
> *and you will find rest for your souls."*
>
> *Jeremiah 6:16*

Those who feared the LORD talked with each other, and the LORD listened and heard. A scroll of remembrance was written in his presence concerning those who feared the LORD and honored his name.

"They will be mine," says the LORD Almighty, "in the day when I make up my treasured possession. I will spare them, just as in compassion a man spares his son who serves him. And you will again see the distinction between the righteous and the wicked, between those who serve God and those who do not."

Malachi 3:16–18

Evil men do not understand justice,
*but those who seek the L*ORD *understand*
it fully.

Proverbs 28:5

Blessed is the man
who does not walk in the counsel
of the wicked
or stand in the way of sinners
or sit in the seat of mockers.
*But his delight is in the law of the L*ORD,
and on his law he meditates
day and night.
He is like a tree planted by streams of water,
which yields its fruit in season
and whose leaf does not wither.
Whatever he does prospers.

Psalm 1:1–3

We continually remember before our God and Father your work produced by faith, your labor prompted by love, and your endurance inspired by hope in our Lord Jesus Christ.

1 Thessalonians 1:3

Devotional Thought on Values

Good parents nurture spiritual values in their children's lives. Although their children are ultimately responsible for accepting the truth of those values, wise parents ... live as examples of authentic faith. They open themselves to spiritual growth and allow their children to observe that process, even if it means exposing their own imperfection and brokenness. They teach their children the tenets of faith—verbally, visually, and metaphorically. They know and use the power of stories in making faith come alive. They gently guide their children into understanding spiritual truth instead of forcing them into rebellion. They do what they can to give their children positive experiences with the church, to portray God's love ... and to show the Christian life as the adventure it can be.

Janis Long Harris

God's Words of Life on

Wisdom

"The fear of the LORD—that is wisdom,
and to shun evil is understanding."
Job 28:28

"I will instruct you and teach you in the way
you should go;
I will counsel you and watch over you,"
says the Lord.
Psalm 32:8

I guide you in the way of wisdom
and lead you along straight paths.
When you walk, your steps will not be hampered;
when you run, you will not stumble.
Proverbs 4:11–12

Jesus said, "Everyone who hears these words of mine and puts them into practice is like a wise man who built his house on the rock. The rain came down, the streams rose, and the winds blew and beat against that house; yet it did not fall, because it had its foundation on the rock."

Matthew 7:24–25

Teach us to number our days aright,
that we may gain a heart of wisdom[, Lord].

Psalm 90:12

Get wisdom, get understanding;
do not forget my words or swerve from them.
Do not forsake wisdom, and she will protect you;
love her, and she will watch over you.
Wisdom is supreme; therefore get wisdom.
Though it cost all you have, get under-
standing.

Proverbs 4:5–7

The fear of the LORD is the beginning of wisdom;
all who follow his precepts have
good understanding.
To him belongs eternal praise.

Psalm 111:10

Trust in the LORD with all your heart
   and lean not on your own understanding;
in all your ways acknowledge him,
   and he will make your paths straight.

Proverbs 3:5–6

Do you not know?
   Have you not heard?
The LORD is the everlasting God,
   the Creator of the ends of the earth.
He will not grow tired or weary,
   and his understanding no one can fathom.
He gives strength to the weary
   and increases the power of the weak.

Isaiah 40:28–29

The wisdom that comes from heaven is first of all
pure; then peace-loving, considerate, submissive, full
of mercy and good fruit, impartial and sincere.

James 3:17

If you accept my words
   and store up my commands within you,
turning your ear to wisdom
   and applying your heart to understanding,
and if you call out for insight
   and cry aloud for understanding,

and if you look for it as for silver
and search for it as for hidden treasure,
then you will understand the fear of the LORD
and find the knowledge of God.
For the LORD gives wisdom,
and from his mouth come knowledge
and understanding.

Proverbs 2:1–6

Where then does wisdom come from?
Where does understanding dwell?
It is hidden from the eyes of every living thing,
concealed even from the birds of the air. . . .
God understands the way to it
and he alone knows where it dwells.

Job 28:20–21, 23

The foolishness of God is wiser than man's wisdom, and
the weakness of God is stronger than man's strength.

1 Corinthians 1:25

Pay attention to my wisdom,
listen well to my words of insight,
that you may maintain discretion
and your lips may preserve knowledge.

Proverbs 5:1–2

*Whoever listens to [wisdom] will live in safety
and be at ease, without fear of harm.*

Proverbs 1:33

If any of you lacks wisdom, he should ask God, who gives generously to all without finding fault, and it will be given to him.

James 1:5

*Man does not comprehend [wisdom's] worth;
it cannot be found in the land of the
living. . . .*
*It cannot be bought with the finest gold,
nor can its price be weighed in silver.*

Job 28:13, 15

*The mouth of the righteous man utters wisdom,
and his tongue speaks what is just.*

Psalm 37:30

*A fool finds pleasure in evil conduct,
but a man of understanding delights in
wisdom.*

Proverbs 10:23

*The fear of the LORD teaches a man wisdom,
and humility comes before honor.*

Proverbs 15:33

By *wisdom a house is built,*
    and through understanding it is estab-
        lished;
through knowledge its rooms are filled
    with rare and beautiful treasures.
                         Proverbs 24:3–4

Know also that wisdom is sweet to your soul;
    if you find it, there is a future hope for you,
    and your hope will not be cut off.
                         Proverbs 24:14

Devotional Thought on Wisdom

God's people breathe cleaner air. And they're healthier because of it. That's what Nehemiah learned while he and a handful of Israelites rebuilt the wall of Jerusalem in fifty-two days.

Nehemiah's enemies were relentless in their hostility. It would have been a simple task, but their conspiracy was their undoing. To conspire means literally *to breathe together.* And these enemies of God breathed each other's anger. They breathed foul air and couldn't think straight.

But that's not why they failed. Praying allowed the people to have fresh insight, to make a wise decision and let Nehemiah lead effectively. There was plenty of fresh air from above.

Our daily breath dare not be amongst ourselves lest the air become stale with our own ideas and prejudices. It would only take one contemptuous soul to foul our thinking.

We must ever be praying—breathing vertically—if we are to have any wisdom from above.

Joni Eareckson Tada

God's Words
OF Life on

Work

Lazy hands make a man poor,
but diligent hands bring wealth.

Proverbs 10:4

Whatever your hand finds to do, do it with all your might.

Ecclesiastes 9:10

He who works his land will have abundant food,
but he who chases fantasies lacks judgment.

Proverbs 12:11

The desires of the diligent are fully satisfied.

Proverbs 13:4

He who gathers money little by little
makes it grow.

Proverbs 13:11

Those who oppose [the Lord's servant] he must gently instruct, in the hope that God will grant them repentance leading them to a knowledge of the truth.

2 Timothy 2:25

And whatever you do, whether in word or deed, do it all in the name of the Lord Jesus, giving thanks to God the Father through him.

Colossians 3:17

God is not unjust; he will not forget your work and the love you have shown him as you have helped his people and continue to help them.

Hebrews 6:10

All hard work brings a profit,
    but mere talk leads only to poverty.

Proverbs 14:23

The laborer's appetite works for him;
    his hunger drives him on.

Proverbs 16:26

The plans of the diligent lead to profit
    as surely as haste leads to poverty.

Proverbs 21:5

Do you see a man skilled in his work?
He will serve before kings;
he will not serve before obscure men.

Proverbs 22:29

My heart took delight in all my work,
and this was the reward for all my labor.

Ecclesiastes 2:10

Sow your seed in the morning,
and at evening let not your hands be idle,
for you do not know which will succeed,
whether this or that,
or whether both will do equally well.

Ecclesiastes 11:6

Make it your ambition to lead a quiet life, to mind your own business and to work with your hands, just as we told you, so that your daily life may win the respect of outsiders and so that you will not be dependent on anybody.

1 Thessalonians 4:11–12

The man who had received the five talents brought the other five. "Master," he said, "you entrusted me with five talents. See, I have gained five more."

His master replied, "Well done, good and faithful servant! You have been faithful with a few things; I will put you in charge of many things. Come and share your master's happiness!"

Matthew 25:20–21

Whatever you do, work at it with all your heart, as working for the Lord, not for men, since you know that you will receive an inheritance from the Lord as a reward. It is the Lord Christ you are serving.

Colossians 3:23–24

May the favor of the Lord our God rest upon us;
establish the work of our hands for us—
yes, establish the work of our hands.
Psalm 90:17

"Six days you shall labor and do all your work, but the seventh day is a Sabbath to the LORD your God. On it you shall not do any work, neither you, nor your son or daughter, nor your manservant or maidservant, nor your ox, your donkey or any of your animals, nor the alien within your gates, so that your manservant and maidservant may rest, as you do," says the Lord.

Deuteronomy 5:13–14

Devotional Thought on Work

As the distributor of the talents, God knows what abilities he has given each individual. It makes sense that we will best do the work that coincides with our God-given talents. So it's important that we try to find out what these are. But how to do it?

It's wise to ask, while we can do something about it, *What is my particular "thing"*? It may be a bent for the technical: business machines and such, a much-in demand skill; or it may be skill in the arts: music, painting, writing, or something else, which also has its place.

God will always make it possible for us to do what he has gifted us to do if we really want his will in our lives.

We need, then, to discover or uncover our talents and put them to work. And one day we will know the ultimate fulfillment: Christ's "well done."

Jeanette Lockerbie

Notes

Notes

Notes

Notes

Notes

Notes

Notes